**European Origins of
American Thought**

D1207684

European Origins of American Thought

Edited by
David D. Van Tassel
Case Western Reserve University
and
Robert W. McAhren
Washington and Lee University

Rand McNally & Company • Chicago

**The Rand McNally Series on
The History of American Thought and Culture**

David D. Van Tassel, editor

Preface

In our present-day preoccupation with the modern world, we too often forget that the colonial history of our country covers a time span only slightly shorter than our national history. We frequently pass over that early period with a few chapters in a textbook or a few lectures, hurriedly trying to get to the more familiar ground of the nineteenth and twentieth centuries. Yet that first century and three-quarters of our existence saw the beginnings of "modern" America. Not the least of the accomplishments of that period was the adaptation of European ideas to an American environment. The assumption of this collection is that American intellectual history had its origins in Europe. America, particularly in its earliest history, was an extension of European culture, and that culture undergirds much of what today we consider to be uniquely American. But a corollary of that assumption is that if Americans drew their ideas from Europe, they also changed them, modified them to fit their circumstances. In the selections included in this book, we have attempted to present at length the writings of *some* Europeans upon whom Americans relied. We have also presented a sampling of the work of American authors, both in order to demonstrate the influence of our Europeans and to show the way in which Americans selected from and modified their European heritage.

The story of the migration of European ideas is presented through parallel documents, linked by a thin thread of narrative, because in this way we are able to introduce the reader directly to the works of men whose ideas are essential to an understanding of the history of American thought, but are not ordinarily considered a part of American history. Thus *European Origins of American Thought* aims to fulfill a major goal of the "History of American Thought and Culture" series, which is to help the general student to perceive and to understand the intellectual and cultural developments during significant periods in American history. It also furnishes background for the other volumes in the series, which are original syntheses embracing chronological periods characterized by a dominant pattern of ideas or important intellectual movements. The selections in this book represent the intellectual and cultural movements of the periods of the Renaissance, Reformation, and Enlightenment. When the reader examines them, we hope that he will not merely note *what* ideas Americans borrowed from Europeans, but consider how and why Americans changed them.

David D. Van Tassel
Robert W. McAhren

Introduction

Traditionally, historians have dated the beginning of modern European history from the fifteenth and sixteenth centuries. They have chosen that period as the end of the Middle Ages and the beginning of modern times because of developments which mark significant new departures: the emergence of a more modern political organization, the beginnings of overseas expansion, and, most of all, the appearance of a movement called the Renaissance in which many see the origins of the "modern mind." The Renaissance had its roots deep in the Middle Ages. In many ways it marked more a shift in emphasis than an embarkation upon something entirely new, yet so dramatic was that shift that, to the eye of the modern observer, it represented the dawn of a new age.

"Renaissance" means "rebirth," and the men of the fifteenth and sixteenth centuries thought that they were experiencing a rebirth of the learning and spirit of classical antiquity. Rejecting the medieval focus upon God, they made man the center of their concern. They viewed the world as a stage on which man could display his talents, rather than a temple where man worshiped God. The medieval crucifix depicted a Godlike Christ serene despite his wounds; the Renaissance crucifix presented Jesus the man, writhing in agony. The medieval artist did not attempt a realistic portrayal of the human figure; it was the meaning behind the picture that was important. The Renaissance exalted the human being; its artists sought to produce an anatomically correct representation of mankind.

Along with the Renaissance came the Reformation. Men imbued with the Renaissance view of man and his world could no longer easily accept the authority of the medieval Church. As the Renaissance sought to revive the civilization of Greece and Rome, so the Reformation sought to restore the early Christian Church before the encrustations of the Middle Ages had altered it. The Reformation was more a revolt against medieval religious practices than against doctrine. When Martin Luther (1483–1546) insisted upon justification by faith alone, he was not so much introducing a new doctrine as rejecting part of the old. Christianity had long accepted the importance of faith; it was the traditional doctrine that faith *and* good works were necessary to salvation that Luther could not abide. Faith yes, but good works no, so far as saving the soul was concerned. Having asserted his essential doctrinal disagreement with the Church, Luther spent much of the rest of his life attacking Church practices: papal authority, the Catholic interpretation of the sacraments, clerical celibacy, monasticism, privileges of the priesthood, and the Latin version of the Bible.

John Calvin (1509–64) ranks next to Luther as a leader of the Reformation. Calvin's *Institutes of the Christian Religion* (1536), with its stress on predestination, was a doctrinal elaboration of Luther's insistence on justification by faith alone. By arguing that God foreordained all that was to happen, Calvin seemed to disregard a basic assumption of the Church, that man had free will. His clear and persuasive reasoning had a great appeal and his teachings spread to most of western Europe and even across the Channel to England. Like Luther before him, Calvin rejected the Middle Ages. Specifically, he discarded the medieval compromise between the spiritual and temporal powers. After a struggle with the secular rulers, the papacy had, at least tacitly, surrendered its claim to superiority over secular government. But at Geneva, where Calvin sought to establish an ideal community, he instituted a theocracy which transformed government into an instrument of theology.

However much the men of the Renaissance and Reformation might reject the institutions of the Middle Ages, there was one practice which none attacked: the union of Church and state. In the Middle Ages when all western Europe enjoyed the luxury of a single church, it was unthinkable that the state should tolerate the religious practices of those whom the Church condemned as schismatics or heretics. Such men the state ostracized—or worse. Luther, however, insisted that every man could interpret the Bible for himself. By denying the necessity of priestly guidance in doctrinal matters, he thus laid the basis for the widespread revolt against the Roman Catholic Church and a continuing fragmentation of Christianity in the Western world. If every man could, in effect, be his own priest, it was inevitable that differences of opinion would arise. Yet the Renaissance state made no more allowance for a variety of sects than had the medieval kingdom. In the Holy Roman Empire the concept of one church and one state was so strong it led to a war between Lutherans and Catholics. The subsequent Peace of Augsburg (1555) granted to each ruler in the empire the right to determine the religion of his subjects. In France civil war also broke out between Catholic and Calvinist (Huguenot) claimants to the throne, resulting in the Edict of Nantes (1598), which gave temporary toleration to the Protestants; it was a short-lived compromise which ended less than a century later. Spain is notorious for her refusal to tolerate either Jew or Protestant.

Calvinism entered England by way of Holland during the reign of Elizabeth I (1558–1603). Although Elizabeth was willing to define her church's position so broadly as to make it possible for both Calvinists and more conservative Christians to remain within the Church of England, she could not conceive of permitting more than one church. Nor could the reformers. The English Calvinists received the name "Puritans" because they wanted to "purify" the Church of England of Catholic vestiges. Their purpose was to reshape the Church so they could remain within it, not to·found a new church. Neither Anglican nor Puritan was willing to give up his ideal of one church for all Englishmen. As Elizabeth's reign drew to a close, the Puritans looked to a new monarch to meet their demands. Only when that monarch, James I (1603–25), proved intent on forcing conformity to Anglican practices which Puritans considered "papistical" did some adopt the alternative of leaving England to found their own community elsewhere. Meanwhile, John Knox introduced Calvinism into Scotland and the Scotch Presbyterians brought it with them when they settled in the middle and southern colonies. The Dutch institutionalized Calvinism in their Reformed Church, which they established in New York. Thus John Calvin's ideas spread up and down the eastern seaboard of North America. Moreover, in many parts of America, in contrast to Europe, they represented the orthodox, established belief, instead of the whimsy of a troublesome minority.

Renaissance humanism manifested itself in many ways. If some aspects of the Renaissance affected the religious life of Europe, still others affected the scientific development of European culture. The Middle Ages had stressed the virtue of a monastic life spent in contemplation of God. The world-view of the sixteenth century encouraged men to leave the monastery and explore the world around them. By the seventeenth century, such explorations had accelerated to the point of producing a new concept of the universe. Not only had Columbus and his followers altered all established terrestrial relationships and doubled the known habitable land, but such men as Copernicus (1473–1543) and Galileo (1564–1642) drastically revised the accepted notions of the earth's place in the solar system. Their work demonstrated that the earth was not the center of the universe, but rather one of a series of planets which revolved about the sun.

At the end of the seventeenth century, an Englishman, Sir Isaac Newton (1642–1727), capped the scientific revolution begun during the Renaissance. In his *Mathematical Principles of Natural Philosophy* (1687), Newton developed a "law" of gravity which provided the keystone of the concept of a universe governed by "natural law." Newton's work had a tremendous impact upon subsequent generations. The world appeared to be a much more orderly place, a place governed by principles which man, using his reason, could discern.

While Newton revolutionized man's view of the cosmos, another Englishman, John Locke (1632–1704), revolutionized man's view of himself. In *An Essay Concerning Human Understanding* (1690), Locke broke with the dominant view of the seventeenth century that man was born with innate ideas implanted by God. Instead, he argued, knowledge was the product of reason's acting upon data absorbed by the senses from the environment. Thus the environment became crucial to the shaping of human behavior. No longer did heredity (or original sin) doom man to live a life of misery. Given the proper environment, man could eliminate evil; change a man's environment and the man himself would change. Or so believed the followers of John Locke.

Taken together, the work of Locke and Newton ushered in a period of intellectual history known as the Enlightenment or Age of Reason. Spurred by Locke and Newton, people developed a tremendous faith in the efficacy of human reason. Newton's apparent solution of some of the most perplexing riddles of the universe led men to conclude that the same methods could solve other problems. They conceived of a static universe, harmonious in all its parts and governed by eternal natural laws which man could discover simply by the use of "right reason." Natural law governed not merely the physical universe but man's social activities, too. In 1776, the Scottish philosopher Adam Smith (1723–90) published *An Inquiry into the Nature and Causes of the Wealth of Nations*, in which he sought to describe the natural laws of economic life.

Reason, once the explicator of authority, became the test of authority. In the Middle Ages faith had preceded reason; men used their reason to explain doctrine which they first accepted on faith. In the eighteenth century, however, men reversed the order: the followers of Enlightened philosophy believed only that which met the test of reason.

Such a world-view had important implications for religion. Newton had made God less necessary. The scientists of the seventeenth century undercut the popular belief that the behavior of the universe was the effect of God's will acting directly upon matter. God ceased to be the immediate cause of all things and became the First Cause. Many now sought to reconcile the new science with the old religion. They argued that Newton simply supported the traditional beliefs of Christians. They found in the "design" of nature not merely the proof of the existence of a Designer, but also of the attributes theologians had long assigned to the Deity on the strength of revelation. Many, however, could not escape the difficulties presented by the problems of reconciling the Bible with a Newtonian universe. How could man believe in a universe governed by natural law and, at the same time, accept the Biblical account of miracles? A minority of English theologians and intellectuals could not and, instead, took God out of His universe and placed Him apart as a disinterested observer. In the early eighteenth century, a few Englishmen very cautiously put forward this view, known as Deism. By the middle of the century it had traveled to France, where its foremost proponent was Voltaire (1694–1778). Yet only in the United States did Deism spread to the common man. While many Americans clung to their older heritage of Calvinism, others, perhaps believing that a new nation founded upon enlightened principles deserved a new, more rational religion, turned to Deism.

Just as the settlers of the seventeenth century brought with them the heritage of the Renaissance and Reformation, so the native-born Americans of the eighteenth century, moved by a genuine interest in ideas and anxious to prove they were as sophisticated as metropolitan Europeans, imported the ideas of the Enlightenment.

Contents

**European Origins of
American Thought**

Chapter I

John Calvin (1509-64)

In 1517, when Martin Luther began the Protestant Reformation, his principal point of doctrinal dispute with the medieval Church was over the role of good works in individual salvation. Luther believed that man was totally dependent upon God's will and that man's own efforts could not save him. All that a man could do was believe in a redeeming Christ. This was the core of the Protestant position: the depravity and helplessness of man. Luther stated his views in a series of polemical pamphlets, rather than in a systematic theological treatise. It was left to another, a Frenchman, John Calvin, to produce the most important doctrinal statement of the Protestant cause.

Calvin financed his education at the University of Paris by taking a minor ecclesiastical post, but his early interests were in the law, not in theological matters. His career at college revealed the bent for clear and persuasive reasoning which was to contribute so much to his later success. Sometime between April, 1532, and November, 1533, Calvin underwent an intense religious experience he later described as a "conversion." His subsequent support of the Lutheran cause forced him to flee the enmity of the French government. Abandoning hope of changing the Church from within, he resigned his ecclesiastical appointments. Fearing his activities now endangered his life, he left France for Basel, Switzerland, a refuge for religious reformers

1

of all types. There he set to work on the first version of the *Institutes of the Christian Religion* (1536).

This great work of a young man only twenty-six years of age had immediate popularity. Its forceful reasoning and clear logic attracted many whom his harsh doctrine might otherwise have repelled.

The same year that he brought forth the *Institutes*, Calvin accepted an invitation to Geneva. There the leaders of reform sought the aid of Calvin's persuasive voice. Yet his advocacy of a rigorously austere manner of living caused such controversy that he eventually had to leave Geneva for the sanctuary of Strasbourg. There he met and married Idelette de Bure, widow of Jean Stordeur, who bore him one child that died a few days after birth. Nine years later its mother followed it to the grave.

In 1541 Calvin returned to a Geneva torn by dissension among the contending religious factions. Gradually, Calvin gained the ascendancy and remodeled Geneva's laws and constitution to fit his theocratic notions of the perfect state. Upon the existing town council he superimposed a "congregation" of clergymen whose responsibility it was to prepare all legislation. A "consistory" of the clergy and twelve elders chosen by the town council supervised the private lives of citizens. Once a year the elders visited the families in their districts and subjected them to a searching inquiry. Spies ferreted out breaches not only of the civil law, but of Calvin's interpretation of the religious law as well. The list of capital crimes included adultery, blasphemy, witchcraft, and heresy. Gambling, dancing, and attending plays brought heavy fines. Attendance at church was compulsory, but the keeping of Christmas was forbidden because it smacked of "popery." Calvin insisted on doctrinal conformity; when Michael Servetus, a Spaniard, disagreed publicly with Calvin on the doctrines of the Trinity, original sin, and baptism, Calvin prosecuted him for heresy and saw him burned to death.

For all the severity of the penalties for disobedience, the records of the Consistory reveal that the citizens of Geneva did not lightly wear their yoke. Their frequent deviations testify to the difficulty of restricting human nature to such an extent. As time went on, however, the most recalcitrant suffered expulsion, leaving the city to Calvin's devoted followers. Gradually Geneva became the focal point of Protestant admiration, and was visited by reform leaders from all over Europe. While Lutheranism remained largely a German and

Scandinavian phenomenon, Calvinism spread throughout Europe and into England and Scotland.

John Calvin: Institutes of the Christian Religion (1536)

God's Government

To represent God as a Creator only for a moment, who entirely finished all his work at once, were frigid and jejune; and in this it behoves us especially to differ from the heathen, that the presence of the Divine power may appear to us no less in the perpetual state of the world than in its first origin. For although the minds even of impious men, by the mere contemplation of earth and heaven, are constrained to rise to the Creator, yet faith has a way peculiar to itself to assign to God the whole praise of creation. To which purpose is that assertion of an Apostle before cited, that it is only "through faith that we understand the worlds were framed by the word of God" (Hebrews xi:3); because, unless we proceed to his providence, we have no correct conception of the meaning of this article, "that God is the Creator;" however we may appear to comprehend it in our minds, and to confess it with our tongues. The carnal sense, when it has once viewed the power of God in the creation, stops there; and when it proceeds the furthest, it only examines and considers the wisdom, and power, and goodness, of the Author in producing such a work, which spontaneously present themselves to the view even of those who are unwilling to observe them. In the next place, it conceives of some general operation of God in preserving and governing it, on which the power of motion depends. Lastly, it supposes that the vigour originally infused by God into all things is sufficient for their sustentation. But faith ought to penetrate further. When it has learned that he is the Creator of all things, it should immediately conclude that he is also their perpetual governor and preserver; and that not by a certain universal motion, actuating the whole machine of the world, and all its

From John Calvin, *Institutes of the Christian Religion,* trans. John Allen, 4th American ed., revised and corrected (Philadelphia: Presbyterian Board of Education, 1843), vol. I, pp. 182–85, 225–27, 305–7, 645–50; vol. II, pp. 144–45, 148–49, 654–57, 660–63.

respective parts, but by a particular providence sustaining, nour-
ishing, and providing for every thing which he has made (Matt.
vi:26; x:29). Thus David, having briefly premised that the world
was made by God, immediately descends to the continual course
of his providence: "By the word of the Lord were the heavens
made; and all the host of them by the breath of his mouth" (Psalm
xxxiii:6). He afterwards adds, "The Lord beholdeth all the sons of
men" (Psalm xxxiii:13); and subjoins more to the same purpose.
For though all men argue not so skilfully, yet, since it would not
be credible that God was concerned about human affairs, if he
were not the Maker of the world, and no one seriously believes
that the world was made by God, who is not persuaded that he
takes care of his own works, it is not without reason that David
conducts us by a most excellent series from one to the other. In
general, indeed, both philosophers teach, and the minds of men
conceive, that all the parts of the world are quickened by the secret
inspiration of God. But they go not so far as David, who is followed by all the pious, when he says, "These all wait upon thee;
that thou mayest give them their meat in due season. That thou
givest them, they gather; thou openest thine hand, they are filled
with good. Thou hidest thy face, they are troubled; thou takest
away their breath, they die, and return to their dust. Thou sendest
forth thy Spirit, they are created; and thou renewest the face of the
earth" (Psalm civ:27–30). Though they subscribe to the assertion
of Paul, that in God "we live, and move, and have our being" (Acts
xvii:28), yet they are very far from a serious sense of his favour,
celebrated by the Apostle; because they have no apprehension of
the special care of God, from which alone his paternal favour is
known.

II. For the clearer manifestation of this difference, it must be
observed that the providence of God, as it is taught in Scripture,
is opposed to fortune and fortuitous accidents. Now, since it has
been the common persuasion in all ages, and is also in the present
day almost the universal opinion, that all things happen fortui-
tously, it is certain that every correct sentiment concerning providence is not only obscured, but almost buried in oblivion by this
erroneous notion. If any one falls into the hands of robbers, or
meets with wild beasts; if by a sudden storm he is shipwrecked on
the ocean; if he is killed by the fall of a house or a tree; if another,
wandering through deserts, finds relief for his penury, or, after

having been tossed about by the waves, reaches the port, and escapes, as it were, but a hair's-breadth from death,—carnal reason will ascribe all these occurrences, both prosperous and adverse, to fortune. But whoever has been taught from the mouth of Christ, that the hairs of his head are all numbered (Matt. x:30), will seek further for a cause, and conclude that all events are governed by the secret counsel of God. And respecting things inanimate, it must be admitted, that, though they are all naturally endued with their peculiar properties, yet they exert not their power, any further than as they are directed by the present hand of God. They are, therefore, no other than instruments into which God infuses as much efficacy as he pleases, bending and turning them to any actions, according to his will. There is no power among all the creatures more wonderful or illustrious, than that of the sun. For, besides his illumination of the whole world by his splendour, how astonishing it is that he cherishes and enlivens all animals with his heat; with his rays inspires fecundity into the earth; from the seeds, genially warmed in her bosom, produces a green herbage, which, being supported by fresh nourishment, he increases and strengthens till it rises into stalks; feeds them with perpetual exhalations, till they grow into blossoms, and from blossoms to fruit, which he then by his influences brings to maturity; that trees, likewise, and vines, by his genial warmth, first put forth leaves, then blossoms, and from the blossoms produce their fruit! But the Lord, to reserve the praise of all these things entirely to himself, was pleased that the light should exist, and the earth abound in every kind of herbs and fruits, before he created the sun. A pious man, therefore, will not make the sun either a principal or necessary cause of those things which existed before the creation of the sun, but only an instrument which God uses, because it is his pleasure so to do; whereas he would find no more difficulty in acting by himself without that luminary. Lastly, as we read that the sun remained in one situation for two days at the prayer of Joshua (Joshua x:13), and that his shadow made a retrograde motion of ten degrees for the sake of king Hezekiah (2 Kings xx:11), God has declared by these few miracles, that the daily rising and setting of the sun is not from a blind instinct of nature, but that he himself governs his course, to renew the memory of his paternal favour towards us. Nothing is more natural than the succession of spring to winter, of summer to spring, and of autumn to summer. But there is so great a diversity and inequality discovered in this series, that it is obvious that every year, month, and day, is governed by a new and particular providence of God.

Original Sin

V. As the spiritual life of Adam consisted in a union to his Maker, so an alienation from him was the death of his soul. Nor is it surprising that he ruined his posterity by his defection, which has perverted the whole order of nature in heaven and earth. "The creatures groan," says Paul, "being made subject to vanity, not willingly" (Rom. viii:20, 22). If the cause be inquired, it is undoubtedly that they sustain part of the punishment due to the demerits of man, for whose use they were created. And his guilt being the origin of that curse which extends to every part of the world, it is reasonable to conclude its propagation to all his offspring. Therefore, when the Divine image in him was obliterated, and he was punished with the loss of wisdom, strength, sanctity, truth, and righteousness, with which he had been adorned, but which were succeeded by the dreadful pests of ignorance, impotence, impurity, vanity, and iniquity, he suffered not alone, but involved all his posterity with him, and plunged them into the same miseries. This is that hereditary corruption which the fathers called *original sin;* meaning by sin, the depravation of a nature previously good and pure; on which subject they had much contention, nothing being more remote from natural reason, than that all should be criminated on account of the guilt of one, and thus his sin become common; which seems to have been the reason why the most ancient doctors of the Church did but obscurely glance at this point, or at least explained it with less perspicuity than it required. Yet this timidity could not prevent Pelagius from arising, who profanely pretended, that the sin of Adam only ruined himself, and did not injure his descendants. By concealing the disease with this delusion, Satan attempted to render it incurable. But when it was evinced by the plain testimony of the Scripture, that sin was communicated from the first man to all his posterity, he sophistically urged that it was communicated by imitation, not by propagation. Therefore good men, and beyond all others Augustine, have laboured to demonstrate that we are not corrupted by any adventitious means, but that we derive an innate depravity from our very birth. The denial of this was an instance of consummate impudence. But the temerity of the Pelagians and Celestians will not appear surprising to him who perceives from the writings of Augustine, what a want of modesty they discover in every thing else. There is certainly no ambiguity in the confession of David, that he was shapen in iniquity, and in sin his mother conceived him (Psalm li:5). He is not there exposing the sins of his mother or of his father; but to enhance his commendations of the Divine goodness towards him, he commences the confession of his depravity from the time of his conception. As it is evident that this was not peculiar to David, it is fairly concluded, that his case exemplifies the common condition of mankind. Every descendant, therefore, from the impure source, is born infected with the contagion of sin; and even before we behold the light of life, we are in sight of God defiled and polluted. For "who can bring a clean thing out of an unclean?" The book of Job tells us, "Not one" (Job xiv:4).

VI. We have heard that the impurity of the parents is so transmitted to the children, that all, without a single exception, are polluted as soon as they exist. But we shall not find the origin of this pollution, unless we ascend to the first parent of us all, as to the fountain which sends forth all the streams. Thus it is certain that Adam was not only the progenitor, but as it were the root of mankind, and therefore that all the race were necessarily vitiated in his corruption. The Apostle explains this by a comparison between him and Christ: "As," says he, "by one man sin entered into the world, and death by sin, and so death passed upon all men, for that all have sinned" (Rom. v:12), so, by the grace of Christ, righteousness and life have been restored to us. . . .

Redemption

The whole human race having perished in the person of Adam, our original excellence and dignity, which we have noticed, so far from being advantageous to us, only involves us in greater ignominy, till God, who does not acknowledge the pollution and corruption of man by sin to be his work, appears as a Redeemer in the person of his only begotten Son. Therefore, since we are fallen from life into death, all that knowledge of God as a Creator, of which we have been treating, would be useless, unless it were succeeded by faith exhibiting God to us as a Father in Christ. This, indeed, was the genuine order of nature, that the fabric of the world should be a school in which we might learn piety, and thence be conducted to eternal life and perfect felicity. But since the fall, withersoever we turn our eyes, the curse of God meets us on every side, which, whilst it seizes innocent creatures and involves them in our guilt, must necessarily overwhelm our souls with despair. For though God is pleased still to manifest his paternal kindness to us in various ways, yet we cannot, from a contemplation of the world, conclude that he is our Father, when our conscience disturbs us within, and convinces us that our sins afford a just reason why God should abandon us, and no longer esteem us as his children. We are also chargeable with stupidity and ingratitude; for our minds, being blinded, do not perceive the truth; and all our senses being corrupted, we wickedly defraud God of his glory. We must therefore subscribe to the declaration of Paul: "For after that in the wisdom of God, the world by wisdom knew not God, it pleased God by the foolishness of preaching to save them that believe" (I Cor. i:21). What he denominates the wisdom of God, is this magnificent theatre of heaven and earth, which is replete with innumerable miracles, and from the contemplation of which we ought wisely to acquire the knowledge of God. But because we have made so little improvement in this way, he recalls us to the faith of Christ, which is despised by unbelievers on account of its apparent folly. Wherefore, though the preaching of the cross is not agreeable to human reason, we ought, nevertheless, to return to God our Creator, from whom we have been alienated, and to have him reassume the character of our Father. Since the fall of the first man, no knowledge of God, without the Mediator, has been available to salvation. For Christ speaks not of his own time only, but comprehends all ages, when he says that "this is life eternal, to know thee, the only true God, and Jesus Christ, whom thou hast sent" (John xvii:3). And this aggravates the stupidity of those who set open the gate of heaven to all unbelievers and profane persons, without the grace of Christ, whom the Scripture universally represents as the only door of entrance into salvation. But if any man would restrict this declaration of Christ to the period of the first promulgation of the gospel, we are prepared with a refutation. For it has been a common opinion, in all ages and nations, that those who are alienated from God, and pronounced accursed, and children of wrath, cannot please him without a reconciliation. Here add the answer of Christ to the woman of Samaria: "Ye worship ye know not what: we know what we worship; for salvation is of the Jews" (John iv:22). In these words he at once condemns all the religions of the Gentiles as false, and assigns a reason for it; because under the law the Redeemer was promised only to the chosen people; whence it follows that no worship has ever been acceptable to God, unless it had respect to Christ. Hence also Paul affirms that all the Gentiles were without God, and destitute of the hope of life (Ephes. ii:12). Now, as John teaches us that life was from the beginning in Christ, and that the whole world are fallen from it (John i:4), it is necessary to return to that fountain; and therefore Christ asserts himself to be the life, as he is the author of the propitiation. And, indeed, the celestial inheritance belongs exclusively to the children of God. But it is very unreasonable that they should be considered in the place and order of his children, who have not been engrafted into the body of his only begotten Son. And John plainly declares that "they who believe in his name become the sons of God" (John i:12). . . .

Predestination

V. Predestination, by which God adopts some to the hope of life, and adjudges others to eternal death, no one, desirous of the credit of piety, dares absolutely to deny. But it is involved in many cavils, especially by those who make foreknowledge the cause of it. We maintain, that both belong to God; but it is preposterous to represent one as dependent on the other. When we attribute foreknowledge to God, we mean that all things have ever been, and perpetually remain, before his eyes, so that to his knowledge nothing is future or past, but all things are present; and present in such a manner, that he does not merely conceive of them from ideas formed in his mind, as things remembered by us appear present to our minds, but really beholds and sees them as if actually placed before him. And this foreknowledge extends to the whole world, and to all the creatures. Predestination we call the eternal decree of God, by which he has determined in himself, what he would have to become of every individual of mankind. For they are not all created with a similar destiny; but eternal life is foreordained for some, and eternal damnation for others. Every man, therefore, being created for one or the other of these ends, we say, he is predestined either to life or to death. . . .

VII. Though it is sufficiently clear, that God, in his secret counsel, freely chooses whom he will, and rejects others, his gratuitous election is but half displayed till we come to particular individuals, to whom God not only offers salvation, but assigns it in such a manner, that the certainty of the effect is liable to no suspense or doubt. These are included in that one seed mentioned by Paul; for though the adoption was deposited in the hand of Abraham, yet many of his posterity being cut off as putrid members, in order to maintain the efficacy and stability of election, it is necessary to ascend to the head, in whom their heavenly Father has bound his elect to each other, and united them to himself by an indissoluble bond. Thus the adoption of the family of Abraham displayed the favour of God, which he denied to others; but in the members of Christ there is a conspicuous exhibition of the superior efficacy of grace; because, being united to their head, they never fail of salvation. Paul, therefore, justly reasons from the passage of Malachi which I have just quoted, that where God, introducing the covenant of eternal life, invites any people to himself, there is a peculiar kind of election as to part of them, so that he does not efficaciously choose all with indiscriminate grace. . . .

. . . That the general election of a people is not always effectual and permanent, a reason readily presents itself, because, when God covenants with them, he does not also give them the spirit of regeneration to enable them to persevere in the covenant to the end; but the external call, without the internal efficacy of grace, which would be sufficient for their preservation, is a kind of medium between the rejection of all mankind and the election of the small number of believers. The whole nation of Israel was called "God's inheritance," though many of them were strangers; but God, having firmly covenanted to be their Father and Redeemer, regards that gratuitous favour rather than the defection of multitudes; by whom his truth was not violated, because his preservation of a certain remnant to himself, made it evident that his calling was without repentance. For God's collection of a Church for himself, from time to time, from the children of Abraham, rather than from the profane nations, was in consideration of his covenant, which, being violated by the multitude, he restricted to a few, to prevent its total failure. Lastly, the general adoption of the seed of Abraham was a visible representation of a greater blessing, which God conferred on a few out of the multitude. This is the reason that Paul so carefully distinguishes the descendants of Abraham according to the flesh, from his spiritual children called after the example of Isaac. Not that the mere descent from Abraham was a vain and unprofitable thing, which could not be asserted without depreciating the covenant; but because to the latter alone the immutable counsel of God, in which he predestinated whom he would, was of itself effectual to salvation. But I advise my readers to adopt no prejudice on either side, till it shall appear from adduced passages of Scripture what sentiments ought to be entertained. In conformity, therefore, to the clear doctrine of the Scripture, we assert, that by an eternal and immutable counsel, God has once for all determined, both whom he would admit to salvation, and whom he would condemn to destruction. We affirm that this counsel, as far as concerns the elect, is founded on his gratuitous mercy, totally irrespective of human merit; but that to those whom he devotes to condemnation, the gate of life is closed by a just and irreprehensible, but incomprehensible, judgment. In the elect, we consider calling as an evidence of election, and justification as another token of its manifestation, till they arrive in glory, which constitutes its completion. As God seals his elect by vocation and justification, so by excluding the reprobate from the knowledge of his name and the sanctification of his Spirit, he affords an indication of the judgment that awaits them. . . .

Present Life

By such principles, the Scripture also fully instructs us in the right use of terrestrial blessings—a thing that ought not to be neglected in a plan for the regulation of life. For if we must live, we must also use the necessary supports of life; nor can we avoid even those things which appear to subserve our pleasures rather than our necessities. It behooves us, therefore, to observe moderation, that we may use them with a pure conscience, whether for necessity or for pleasure. This the Lord prescribes in his word, when he teaches us, that to his servants the present life is like a pilgrimage, in which they are travelling towards the celestial kingdom. If we are only to pass through the earth, we ought undoubtedly to make such a use of its blessings as will rather assist than retard us in our journey. It is not without reason, therefore, that Paul advises us to use this world as though we used it not, and to buy with the same disposition with which we sell (I Cor. vii:30, 31). But as this is a difficult subject, and there is danger of falling into one of two opposite errors, let us endeavour to proceed on safe ground, that we may avoid both extremes. For there have been some, in other respects good and holy men, who, seeing that intemperance and luxury, unless restrained with more than ordinary severity, would perpetually indulge the most extravagant excesses, and desiring to correct such a pernicious evil, have adopted the only method which occurred to them, by permitting men to use corporeal blessings no further than their necessity should absolutely require. This advice was well intended, but they were far too austere. For they committed the very dangerous error of imposing on the conscience stricter rules than those which are prescribed to it by the word of the Lord. By restriction within the demands of necessity, they meant an abstinence from every thing from which it is possible to abstain; so that, according to them, it would scarcely be lawful to eat or drink any thing but bread and water. Others have discovered still greater austerity, like Crates the Theban, who is said to have thrown his wealth into the sea, from an apprehension that, unless it were destroyed, he should himself be destroyed by it. On the contrary, many in the present day, who seek a pretext to excuse intemperance in the use of external things, and at the same time desire to indulge the licentiousness of the flesh, assume as granted, what I by no means concede to them, that this liberty is not to be restricted by any limitation; but that it ought to be left to the conscience of every individual to use as much as he thinks lawful for himself. I grant, indeed, that it is neither right nor possible to bind the conscience with the fixed and precise rules of law in this case; but since the Scripture delivers general rules for the lawful use of earthly things, our practice ought certainly to be regulated by them.

II. It must be laid down as a principle, that the use of the gifts of God is not erroneous when it is directed to the same end for which the Creator himself has created and appointed them for us; since he has created them for our benefit, not for our injury. Wherefore, no one will observe a more proper rule, than he who shall diligently regard this end. Now, if we consider for what end he has created the various kinds of aliment, we shall find that he intended to provide not only for our necessity, but likewise for our pleasure and delight. So in clothing, he has had in view not mere necessity, but propriety and decency. In herbs, trees, and fruits, besides their various uses, his design has been to gratify us by graceful forms and pleasant odours. For if this were not true, the Psalmist would not account among the Divine blessings, "wine that maketh glad the heart of man, and oil to make his face to shine" (Psalm civ:15); nor would the Scriptures universally declare, in commendation of his goodness, that he has given all these things to men. And even the natural properties of things sufficiently indicate for what end, and to what extent, it is lawful to use them. But shall the Lord have endued flowers with such beauty, to present itself to our eyes, with such sweetness of smell, to impress our sense of smelling; and shall it be unlawful for our eyes to be affected with the beautiful sight, or our olfactory nerves with the agreeable odour? What! has he not made such a distinction of colours as to render some more agreeable than others? Has he not given to gold and silver, to ivory and marble, a beauty which makes them more precious than other metals or stones? In a word, has he not made many things worthy of our estimation, independently of any necessary use?

III. Let us discard, therefore, that inhuman philosophy which, allowing no use of the creatures but what is absolutely necessary, not only malignantly deprives us of the lawful enjoyment of the Divine beneficence, but which cannot be embraced till it has despoiled man of all his senses, and reduced him to a senseless block. But, on the other hand, we must, with equal diligence, oppose the licentiousness of the flesh; which unless it be rigidly restrained, transgresses every bound. And, as I have observed, it has its advocates, who, under the pretext of liberty, allow it every thing. In the first place, it will be one check to it, if it be concluded, that all things are made for us, in order that we may know and acknowledge their Author, and celebrate his goodness towards us by giving him thanks. What will become of thanksgiving, if you overcharge yourself with dainties or wine, so as to be stupefied or rendered unfit for the duties of piety and the business of your station? Where is any acknowledgment of God, if your body in consequence of excessive abundance, being inflamed with the vilest passions, infects the mind with its impurity, so that you cannot discern what is right or virtuous? Where is gratitude towards God for clothing, if, on account of our sumptuous apparel, we admire ourselves and despise others? if with the elegance and beauty of it, we prepare ourselves for unchastity? Where is our acknowledgment of God, if our minds be fixed on the splendour of our garments? For many so entirely devote all their senses to the pursuit of pleasure, that the mind is, as it were, buried in it; many are so delighted with marble, gold, and pictures, that they become like statues, are, as it were, metamorphosed into metal, and resemble painted images. The flavour of meats, or the sweetness of odours, so stupefies some, that they have no relish for any thing spiritual. The same may be observed in other cases. Wherefore it is evident, that this principle lays some restraint on the license of abusing the Divine bounties, and confirms the rule given us by Paul, that we "make not provision for the flesh, to fulfil the lusts thereof" (Rom. xiii:14); which, if they are allowed too much latitude, will transgress all the bounds of temperance and moderation.

IV. But there is no way more certain or concise than what we derive from a contempt of the present life, and meditation on a heavenly immortality. For thence follow two rules. The first is, "that they that have wives be as though they had none; and they that buy, as though they possessed not; and they that use this world, as not abusing it" (I Cor. vii:29, 30, 31); according to the direction of Paul: the second, that we should learn to bear penury with tranquillity and patience, as well as to enjoy abundance with moderation. He who commands us to use this world as though we used it not, prohibits not only all intemperance in eating and drinking, and excessive delicacy, ambition, pride, haughtiness, and fastidiousness in our furniture, our habitations, and our apparel, but every care and affection, which would either seduce or disturb us from thoughts of the heavenly life, and attention to the improvement of our souls. Now, it was anciently and truly observed by Cato, That there is a great concern about adorning the body, and a great carelessness about virtue; and it is an old proverb, That they who are much engaged in the care of the body, are generally negligent of the soul. Therefore, though the liberty of believers in external things cannot be reduced to certain rules, yet it is evidently subject to this law, That they should indulge themselves as little as possible; that, on the contrary, they should perpetually and resolutely exert themselves to retrench all superfluities and to restrain luxury;

and that they should diligently beware lest they pervert into impediments things which were given for their assistance.

V. The other rule will be, That persons whose property is small should learn to be patient under their privations, that they may not be tormented with an immoderate desire of riches. They who observe this moderation, have attained no small proficiency in the school of the Lord, as he who has made no proficiency in this point can scarcely give any proof of his being a disciple of Christ. For besides that an inordinate desire of earthly things is accompanied by most other vices, he who is impatient under penury, in abundance generally betrays the opposite passion. By this I mean, that he who is ashamed of a mean garment, will be proud of a splendid one; he who, not content with a slender meal, is disquieted with the desire of a more sumptuous one, would also intemperately abuse those dainties, should they fall to his lot; he who bears a private and mean condition with discontent and disquietude, would not abstain from pride and arrogance, should he rise to eminence and honours. Let all, therefore, who are sincere in the practice of piety, earnestly endeavour to learn, after the apostolic example, "both to be full and to be hungry, both to abound and to suffer need" (Phil. iv:12). The Scripture has also a third rule, by which it regulates the use of earthly things; of which something was said, when we treated of the precepts of charity. For it states, that while all these things are given to us by the Divine goodness, and appointed for our benefit, they are, as it were, deposits intrusted to our care, of which we must one day give an account. We ought, therefore, to manage them in such a manner that this alarm may be incessantly sounding in our ears, "Give an account of thy stewardship" (Luke xvi:2). Let it also be remembered by whom this account is demanded; that it is by him who has so highly recommended abstinence, sobriety, frugality, and modesty; who abhors profusion, pride, ostentation, and vanity; who approves of no other management of his blessings, than such as is connected with charity; who has with his own mouth already condemned all those pleasures which seduce the heart from chastity and purity, or tend to impair the understanding.

VI. Lastly, it is to be remarked, that the Lord commands every one of us, in all the actions of life, to regard his vocation. For he knows with what great inquietude the human mind is inflamed, with what desultory levity it is hurried hither and thither, and how insatiable is its ambition to grasp different things at once. Therefore, to prevent universal confusion being produced by our folly and temerity, he has appointed to all their particular duties in different spheres of life. And that no one might rashly transgress the limits prescribed, he has styled such spheres of life *vocations*, or *callings*. Every individual's line of life, therefore, is, as it were, a post assigned him by the Lord, that he may not wander about in uncertainty all his days. And so necessary is this distinction, that in his sight all our actions are estimated according to it, and often very differently from the sentence of human reason and philosophy. There is no exploit esteemed more honourable, even among philosophers, than to deliver our country from tyranny; but the voice of the celestial Judge openly condemns the private man who lays violent hands on a tyrant. It is not my design, however, to stay to enumerate examples. It is sufficient if we know that the principle and foundation of right conduct in every case is the vocation of the Lord, and that he who disregards it will never keep the right way in the duties of his station. He may sometimes, perhaps, achieve something apparently laudable; but however it may appear in the eyes of men, it will be rejected at the throne of God; besides which, there will be no consistency between the various parts of his life. Our life, therefore, will then be best regulated, when it is directed to this mark; since no one will be impelled by his own temerity to attempt more than is compatible with his calling, because he will know that it is unlawful to transgress the bounds assigned him. He that is in obscurity will lead a private life without discontent, so as not to desert the station in which God has placed him. It will also be no small alleviation of his cares, labours, troubles, and other burdens, when a man knows that in all these things he has God for his guide. The magistrate will execute his office with greater pleasure, the father of a family will confine himself to his duty with more satisfaction, and all, in their respective spheres of life, will bear and surmount the inconveniences, cares, disappointments, and anxieties which befall them, when they shall be persuaded that every individual has his burden laid upon him by God. Hence also will arise peculiar consolation, since there will be no employment so mean and sordid (provided we follow our vocation) as not to appear truly respectable, and be deemed highly important in the sight of God.

Civil Government

XXII. The first duty of subjects towards their magistrates is to entertain the most honourable sentiments of their function, which they know to be a jurisdiction delegated to them from God, and on that account to esteem and reverence them as God's ministers and viceregents. For there are some persons to be found, who show themselves very obedient to their magistrates, and have not the least wish that there were no magistrates for them to obey, because they know them to be so necessary to the public good; but who, nevertheless, consider the magistrates themselves as no other than necessary evils. But something more than this is required of us by Peter, when he commands us to "honour the king" (1 Peter ii:17); and by Solomon, when he says, "Fear thou the Lord and the king" (Prov. xxiv:21); for Peter, under the term *honour*, comprehends a sincere and candid esteem; and Solomon, by connecting the king with the Lord, attributes to him a kind of sacred veneration and dignity. It is also a remarkable commendation of magistrates which is given by Paul, when he says, that we "must needs be subject, not only for wrath, but also for conscience sake" (Rom. xiii:5); by which he means, that subjects ought to be induced to submit to princes and governors, not merely from a dread of their power, as persons are accustomed to yield to an armed enemy, who they know will immediately take vengeance upon them if they resist; but because the obedience which is rendered to princes and magistrates is rendered to God, from whom they have received their authority. I am not speaking of the persons, as if the mask of dignity ought to palliate or excuse folly, ignorance, or cruelty, and conduct the most nefarious and flagitious, and so to acquire for vices the praise due to virtues; but I affirm that the station itself is worthy of honour and reverence; so that, whoever our governors are, they ought to possess our esteem and veneration on account of the office which they fill.

XXIII. Hence follows another duty, that, with minds disposed to honour and reverence magistrates, subjects approve their obedience to them, in submitting to their edicts, in paying taxes, in discharging public duties, and bearing burdens which relate to the common defence, and in fulfilling all their other commands. . . .

. . . Here let no man deceive himself. For as it is impossible to

resist the magistrate without, at the same time, resisting God himself; though an unarmed magistrate may seem to be despised with
impunity, yet God is armed to inflict exemplary vengeance on the
contempt offered to himself. Under this obedience I also include
the moderation which private persons ought to prescribe to themselves in relation to public affairs, that they do not, without being
called upon, intermeddle with affairs of state, or rashly intrude
themselves into the office of magistrates, or undertake any thing of
a public nature. If there be any thing in the public administration
which requires to be corrected, let them not raise any tumults, or
take the business into their own hands, which ought to be all bound
in this respect, but let them refer it to the cognizance of the magistrate, who is alone authorized to regulate the concerns of the
public. I mean, that they ought to attempt nothing without being
commanded; for when they have the command of a governor, then
they also are invested with public authority. For, as we are accustomed to call the counsellors of a prince *his eyes and ears*, so they
may not unaptly be called *his hands* whom he has commissioned to
execute his commands.

XXIV. Now, as we have hitherto described a magistrate who
truly answers to his title; who is the father of his country, and, as
the poet calls him, the pastor of his people, the guardian of peace,
the protector of justice, the avenger of innocence; he would justly
be deemed insane who disapproved of such a government. But,
as it has happened, in almost all ages, that some princes, regardless
of every thing to which they ought to have directed their attention
and provision, give themselves up to their pleasures in indolent
exemption from every care; others, absorbed in their own interest,
expose to sale all laws, privileges, rights, and judgments; others
plunder the public of wealth, which they afterwards lavish in
mad prodigality; others commit flagrant outrages, pillaging houses,
violating virgins and matrons, and murdering infants; many persons cannot be persuaded that such ought to be acknowledged as
princes, who, as far as possible, they ought to obey. For in such
enormities, and actions so completely incompatible, not only with
the office of a magistrate, but with the duty of every man, they discover no appearance of the image of God, which ought to be conspicuous in a magistrate; while they perceive no vestige of that
minister of God who is "not a terror to good works, but to the evil,"
who is sent "for the punishment of evil-doers, and for the praise of

them that do well;" nor recognize that governor, whose dignity and authority the Scripture recommends to us. And certainly the minds of men have always been naturally disposed to hate and execrate tyrants as much as to love and reverence legitimate kings.

XXV. But, if we direct our attention to the word of God, it will carry us much further; even to submit to the government, not only of those princes who discharge their duty to us with becoming integrity and fidelity, but of all who possess the sovereignty, even though they perform none of the duties of their function. For, though the Lord testifies that the magistrate is an eminent gift of his liberality to preserve the safety of men, and prescribes to magistrates themselves the extent of their duty, yet he at the same time declares, that whatever be their characters, they have their government only from him; that those who govern for the public good are true specimens and mirrors of his beneficence; and that those who rule in an unjust and tyrannical manner are raised up by him to punish the iniquity of the people; that all equally possess that sacred majesty with which he has invested legitimate authority.

. . .

XXIX. Finally, we owe these sentiments of affection and reverence to all our rulers, whatever their characters may be; which I the more frequently repeat, that we may learn not to scrutinize the persons themselves, but may be satisfied with knowing that they are invested by the will of the Lord with that function, upon which he has impressed an inviolable majesty. But it will be said, that rulers owe mutual duties to their subjects. That I have already confessed. But he who infers from this that obedience ought to be rendered to none but just rulers, is a very bad reasoner. For husbands owe mutual duties to their wives, and parents to their children. Now, if husbands and parents violate their obligations; if parents conduct themselves with discouraging severity and fastidious moroseness towards their children, whom they are forbidden to provoke to wrath (Ephes. vi:1; Col. iii:21); if husbands despise and vex their wives, whom they are commanded to love and to spare as the weaker vessels (Ephes. v:25; 1 Pet. iii:7); does it follow that children should be less obedient to their parents, or wives to their husbands? They are still subject, even to those who are wicked and unkind. As it is incumbent on all, not to inquire into the duties of one another, but to confine their attention respectively to their own, this consideration ought particularly to be regarded by those who are subject to the authority of others. Wherefore, if we are inhumanly harassed by a cruel prince; if we are rapaciously plundered by an avaricious or luxurious one; if we are neglected by an indolent one; or if we are persecuted, on account of piety, by an impious and sacrilegious one,—let us first call to mind our transgressions against God, which he undoubtedly chastises by these scourges. Thus our impatience will be restrained by humility. Let us, in the next place, consider that it is not our province to remedy these evils; and that nothing remains for us, but to implore the aid of the Lord, in whose hand are the hearts of kings and the revolutions of kingdoms. It is "God" who "standeth in the congregation of the mighty," and "judgeth among the gods" (Psalm lxxxii:1); whose presence shall confound and crush all kings and judges of the earth who shall not have kissed his Son (Psalm ii:10–12); "that decree unrighteous decrees, to turn aside the needy from judgment, and to take away the right from the poor, that widows may be their prey, and that they may rob the fatherless" (Isaiah x:1, 2).

XXX. And here is displayed his wonderful goodness, and power, and providence; for sometimes he raises up some of his servants as public avengers, and arms them with his commission to punish unrighteous domination, and to deliver from their distressing calamities a people who have been unjustly oppressed: sometimes he accomplishes this end by the fury of men who meditate and attempt something altogether different. Thus he liberated the people of Israel from the tyranny of Pharaoh by Moses; from the oppression of Chusan by Othniel; and from other yokes by other kings and judges. Thus he subdued the pride of Tyre by the Egyptians; the insolence of the Egyptians by the Assyrians; the haughtiness of the Assyrians by the Chaldeans; the confidence of Babylon by the Medes and Persians, after Cyrus had subjugated the Medes. The ingratitude of the kings of Israel and Judah, and their impious rebellion, notwithstanding his numerous favours, he repressed and punished, sometimes by the Assyrians, sometimes by the Babylonians. These were all the executioners of his vengeance, but not all in the same manner. The former, when they were called forth to the performance of such acts by a legitimate commission from God, in taking arms against kings, were not chargeable with the least violation of that majesty with which kings are invested by the ordination of God; but, being armed with authority from Heaven, they punished an inferior power by a superior one, as it is lawful for kings to punish their inferior officers. The latter, though they were guided by the hand of God in such directions as he pleased, and performed his work without being conscious of it, nevertheless contemplated in their hearts nothing but evil.

XXXI. But whatever opinion be formed of the acts of men, yet the Lord equally executed his work by them, when he broke the sanguinary sceptres of insolent kings, and overturned tyrannical governments. Let princes hear and fear. But, in the mean while, it behoves us to use the greatest caution, that we do not despise or violate that authority of magistrates, which is entitled to the greatest veneration, which God has established by the most solemn commands, even though it reside in those who are most unworthy of it, and who, as far as in them lies, pollute it by their iniquity. For though the correction of tyrannical domination is the vengeance of God, we are not, therefore, to conclude that it is committed to us, who have received no other command than to obey and suffer. This observation I always apply to private persons. For if there be, in the present day, any magistrates appointed for the protection of the people and the moderation of the power of kings, such as were, in ancient times, the Ephori, who were a check upon the kings among the Lacedæmonians, or the popular tribunes upon the consuls among the Romans, or the Demarchi upon the senate among the Athenians; or with power such as perhaps is now possessed by the three estates in every kingdom when they are assembled; I am so far from prohibiting them, in the discharge of their duty, to oppose the violence or cruelty of kings, that I affirm, that if they connive at kings in their oppression of their people, such forbearance involves the most nefarious perfidy, because they fraudulently betray the liberty of the people, of which they know that they have been appointed protectors by the ordination of God.

XXXII. But in the obedience which we have shown to be due to the authority of governors, it is always necessary to make one exception, and that is entitled to our first attention,—that it do not seduce us from obedience to him, to whose will the desires of all kings ought to be subject, to whose decrees all their commands ought to yield, to whose majesty all their sceptres ought to submit. And, indeed, how preposterous it would be for us, with a view to satisfy men, to incur the displeasure of him on whose account we yield obedience to men! The Lord, therefore, is the King of kings; who, when he has opened his sacred mouth, is to be heard alone, above all, for all, and before all; in the next place, we are subject to those men who preside over us; but no otherwise than in him. If they command any thing against him, it ought not to have the least attention; nor, in this case, ought we to pay any regard to all that dignity attached to magistrates; to which no injury is done when it is subjected to the unrivalled and supreme power of God. On this principle Daniel denied that he had committed any crime against the king in disobeying his impious decree (Dan. vi:22); because the king had exceeded the limits of his office, and had not only done an injury to men, but, by raising his arm against God, had degraded his own authority. On the other hand, the Israelites are condemned for having been too submissive to the impious edict of their king. For when Jeroboam had made his golden calves, in compliance with his will, they deserted the temple of God and revolted to new superstitions. Their posterity conformed to the decrees of their idolatrous kings with the same facility. The prophet severely condemns them for having "willingly walked after the commandment" (Hos. v:11): so far is any praise from being due to the pretext of humility, with which courtly flatterers excuse themselves and deceive the unwary, when they deny that it is lawful for them to refuse compliance with any command of their kings; as if God had resigned his right to mortal men when he made them rulers of mankind; or as if earthly power were diminished by being subordinated to its author, before whom even the principalities of heaven tremble with awe. I know what great and present danger awaits this constancy, for kings cannot bear to be disregarded without the greatest indignation; and "the wrath of a king," says Solomon, "is as messengers of death" (Prov. xvi:14). But since this edict has been proclaimed by that celestial herald, Peter, "We ought to obey God rather than men" (Acts v:29),—let us console ourselves with this thought, that we truly perform the obedience which God requires of us, when we suffer any thing rather than deviate from piety. And that our hearts may not fail us, Paul stimulates us with another consideration—that Christ has redeemed us at the immense price which our redemption cost him, that we may not be submissive to the corrupt desires of men, much less be slaves to their impiety (1 Cor. vii:23).

Saybrook Synod: Declaration of Faith (1680)

During the seventeenth century, English Puritans, Scottish Presbyterians, and members of the Dutch Reformed Church spread Calvinistic ideas all along the eastern seaboard of the North American continent. Admittedly it was a Calvinism modified by successive generations of interpreters, but nonetheless it clearly harked back to the magnum opus of that young lawyer of the sixteenth century. There were copies of the *Institutes* in the earliest colonial libraries, including the one John Harvard donated to the institution destined to bear his name. Puritan New England's inhabitants frequently consulted the master, although probably few shared the enthusiasm of John Cotton, who liked to "sweeten his mouth with a bit of Calvin" before retiring. The following excerpts from the *Declaration of Faith* adopted by two New England synods in 1680 are clear evidence of the Genevan's influence upon the New England ministry.

Of Providence

God the great Creator of all things, doth uphold, direct, dispose and govern all creatures, actions and things from the greatest even to the least by his most wise and holy Providence, according unto his infallible fore-knowledge, and the free and immutable counsel of his own Will, to the praise of the glory of his Wisdom, Power, Justice, Goodness and Mercy.

II. Although in relation to the fore-knowledge and decree of God, the first Cause, all things come to pass immutably and infallibly; yet by the same Providence he ordereth them to fall out, according to the nature of second Causes, either necessarily, freely, or contingently.

III. God in his ordinary Providence maketh use of Means, yet is free to work without, above, and against them at his pleasure.

IV. The almighty Power, unsearchable Wisdom, and infinite Goodness of God, so far manifest themselves in his Providence, in that his determinate Counsel extendeth it self even to the first Fall, and all other sins of Angels and Men (and that not by a bare permission) which also he most wisely and powerfully boundeth,

From Williston Walker, ed., *The Creeds and Platforms of Congregationalism* (New York: Charles Scribner, 1893), pp. 372–75, 377–78.

and otherwise ordereth and governeth in a manifold Dispensation to his own most holy ends; yet so, as the sinfulness thereof proceedeth onely from the Creature, and not from God, who being most holy and righteous, neither is, nor can be the author or approver of sin.

V. The most wise, righteous and gracious God doth oftentimes leave for a season his own children to manifold temptations, and the corruption of their own hearts, to chastise them for their former sins, or to discover unto them the hidden strength of corruption, and deceitfulness of their hearts, that they may be humbled; and to raise them to a more close and constant dependence for their support upon himself, and to make them more watchful against all future occasions of sin, and for sundry other just and holy ends.

VI. As for those wicked and ungodly men, whom God as a righteous Judge, for former sins, doth blinde and harden, from them he not onely withholdeth his grace, whereby they might have been inlightened in their understandings, and wrought upon in their hearts; but sometimes also withdraweth the gifts which they had, and exposeth them to such objects, as their corruption makes occasions of sin; and withal gives them over to their own lusts, the temptations of the world, and the power of Satan; whereby it comes to pass that they harden themselves, even under those means which God useth for the softning of others.

VII. As the Providence of God doth in general reach to all Creatures, so after a most special maner it taketh care of his Church, and disposeth all things to the good thereof.

Of the Fall of Man, of Sin, and of the Punishment Thereof

God having made a Covenant of Works and Life, thereupon, with our first parents and all their posterity in them, they being seduced by the subtilty and temptation of Satan did wilfully transgress the Law of their Creation, and break the Covenant in eating the forbidden fruit.

II. By this sin they, and we in them, fell from original righteousness and communion with God, and so became dead in sin, and wholly defiled in all the faculties and parts of soul and body.

III. They being the Root, and by God's appointment standing in the room and stead of all mankinde, the guilt of this sin was imputed, and corrupted nature conveyed to all their posterity descending from them by ordinary generation.

IV. From this Original corruption, whereby we are utterly indisposed, disabled and made opposite to all good, and wholly enclined to all evil, do proceed all Actual transgressions.

V. This Corruption of nature during this life, doth remain in those that are regenerated; and although it be through Christ pardoned and mortified, yet both it self and all the motions thereof are truely and properly sin.

VI. Every sin, both original and actual, being a transgression of the righteous Law of God, and contrary thereunto, doth in its own nature bring guilt upon the sinner, whereby he is bound over to the wrath of God, and curse of the Law, and so made subject to death, with all miseries, spiritual, temporal and eternal.

Of God's Covenant with Man

The distance between God and the Creature is so great, that although reasonable creatures do owe obedience unto him as their Creator, yet they could never have attained the reward of life, but by some voluntary condescension on God's part, which he hath been pleased to express by way of Covenant.

II. The first Covenant made with man, was a Covenant of Works, wherein life was promised to Adam, and in him to his posterity, upon condition of perfect and personal obedience.

III. Man by his fall having made himself uncapable of life by that Covenant, the Lord was pleased to make a second, commonly called the Covenant of Grace; wherein he freely offereth unto sinners life and salvation by Jesus Christ, requiring of them faith in him that they may be saved, and promising to give unto all those that are ordained unto life, his holy Spirit, to make them willing and able to believe.

IV. This Covenant of Grace is frequently set forth in the Scripture by the name of a Testament, in reference to the death of Jesus Christ the Testator, and to the everlasting Inheritance, with all things belonging to it, therein bequeathed.

V. Although this Covenant hath been differently and variously administred in respect of Ordinances and Institutions in the time of the Law, and since the coming of Christ in the flesh; yet for the substance and efficacy of it, to all its spirit and saving ends, it is one and the same; upon the account of which various dispensations, it is called the Old and New Testament.

Of Free-will

God hath endued the Will of man with that natural liberty and power of acting upon choice, that it is neither forced, nor by any absolute necessity of Nature determined to do good or evil.

II. Man in his state of Innocency had freedom and power to will and to do that which was good and well pleasing to God; but yet mutably, so that he might fall from it.

III. Man by his fall into a state of sin, hath wholly lost all ability of will to any spiritual good accompanying salvation; so as a natural man being altogether averse from that good, and dead in sin, is not able by his own strength to convert himself, or to prepare himself thereunto.

IV. When God converts a sinner, and translates him into the state of grace, he freeth him from his natural bondage under sin, and by his grace alone inables him freely to will and to do that which is spiritually good; yet so, as that by reason of his remaining corruption, he doth not perfectly nor onely will that which is good, but doth also will that which is evil.

V. The will of man is made perfectly and immutably free to good alone in the state of Glory onely.

Michael Wigglesworth: Day of Doom (1662)

Calvin's influence pervaded even the literature produced in seventeenth-century New England. The following selection is from a famous poem, *The Day of Doom* (1662), by Michael Wigglesworth (1631–1705), graduate of Harvard and a Puritan divine.

> All silence keep, both Goats and Sheep,
>   before the Judge's Throne;
> With mild aspect to his Elect
>   then spake the Holy One;

From Michael Wigglesworth, *The Day of Doom* (New York: American News Co., 1867), pp. 32–35.

My Sheep draw near, your Sentence hear,
 which is to you no dread,
Who clearly now discern, and know
 your sins are pardoned.

'Twas meet that ye should judged be,
 that so the world may spy
No cause of grudge, when as I Judge
 and deal impartially.
Know therefore all, both great and small,
 the ground and reason why
These Men do stand at my right hand,
 and look so chearfully.

These Men be those my Father chose
 before the worlds foundation,
And to me gave, that I should save
 from Death and Condemnation.
For whose dear sake I flesh did take,
 was of a Woman born,
And did inure my self t' indure,
 unjust reproach and scorn.

For them it was that I did pass
 through sorrows many one:
That I drank up that bitter Cup,
 which made me sigh and groan.
The Cross his pain I did sustain;
 yea more, my Fathers ire
I underwent, my Blood I spent
 to save them from Hell fire.

Thus I esteem'd, thus I redeem'd
 all these from every Nation,
That they may be (as now you see)
 a chosen Generation.
What if ere-while they were as vile,
 and bad as any be,
And yet from all their guilt and thrall
 at once I set them free?

My grace to one is wrong to none:
    none can Election claim,
Amongst all those their souls that lose,
    none can Rejection blame.
He that may chuse, or else refuse,
    all men to save or spill,
May this Man chuse, and that refuse,
    redeeming whom he will.

But as for those whom I have chose
    Salvation heirs to be,
I underwent their punishment,
    and therefore set them free;
I bore their grief, and their relief
    by suffering procur'd,
That they of bliss and happiness
    might firmly be assur'd.

And this my grace they did imbrace,
    believing on my Name;
Which Faith was true, the fruits do shew
    proceeding from the same:
Their Penitence, their Patience,
    their Love and Self-denial
In suffering losses, and bearing Crosses,
    when put upon the tryal.

Their sin forsaking, their chearful taking
    my yoke, their Charity
Unto the Saints in all their wants,
    and in them unto me,
These things do clear, and make appear
    their Faith to be unfaigned,
And that a part in my desert
    and purchase they have gained.

Their debts are paid, their peace is made,
    their sins remitted are;
Therefore at once I do pronounce,
    and openly declare

That Heav'n is theirs, that they be Heirs
    of Life and of Salvation!
Nor ever shall they come at all
    to Death or to Damnation.

Come, Blessed Ones, and sit on Thrones,
    Judging the World with me:
Come, and possess your happiness,
    and bought felicitie.
Henceforth no fears, no care, no tears,
    no sin shall you annoy,
Nor any thing that grief doth bring:
    Eternal Rest enjoy.

You bore the Cross, you suffered loss
    of all for my Names sake:
Receive the Crown that's now your own;
    come, and a Kingdom take.
Thus spake the Judge; the wicked grudge,
    and grind their teeth in vain;
They see with groans these plac't on Thrones
    which addeth to their pain:

That those whom they did wrong and slay,
    must now their judgment see!
Such whom they slighted, and once despighted,
    must now their Judges be!
Thus 'tis decreed, such is their meed,
    and guerdon glorious!
With Christ they sit, Judging is fit
    to plague the Impious.

Increase Mather:
Awakening Truths Tending to Conversion (1710)

Calvinism raised many serious practical problems when men sought
to apply it to human behavior. Perhaps the most serious was com-
bating the hopelessness which predestination created in the minds of
"sinners" who could not meet the Puritan test for acceptance as a
member of God's "visible" elect. In the following selection, Increase

Mather (1639–1723), a second-generation New Englander and one of the most famous Puritan ministers, grappled with this problem.

Predestination and Human Exertions

1. I say, God is not bound to give Sinners Grace: He is an absolute Sovereign, and may give Grace or deny Grace to whom he pleaseth. Shall the thing formed, say to him that formed it, why hast thou made me thus? has not the Potter power over the Clay, to make one vessel unto honour, and another to dishonour? The glorious God has a greater power over his Creatures, than the Potter has over the Clay. Wherefore, *He has Mercy on whom He will have Mercy, and whom He will He hardens*, Rom. 9. 18. If He giveth Grace to any man in the World, it is from His Sovereign good pleasure. Why were such poor Fishermen as *Peter*, and *James*, and *John*, and others, as mean as they, made the Subjects of Saving Grace, when many incomparably beyond them in Learning and Wisdom, have been left to perish in their unbelief? Even so, because so it has seemed good in the sight of Him, who is the Lord of Heaven and Earth, *Math.* 11. 25, 26. Grace is a wonderful gift of God. Sinners are enemies to him, and Rebels against him: Is He bound to bestow such a gift on his Enemies, when it may be too they will not so much as humbly Pray unto him for it[?] Indeed He sometimes has done so. Sinners that never Prayed to him, that never had one thought in their hearts of returning to him, he has miraculously Prevented them with Sovereign Grace. So it was with the Converted Gentiles. Of them the Lord sayes, *I am sought of them that asked not for me, I am found of them that sought me not, I said, behold me, behold me to a Nation that was not called by my Name*, Isa. 69. 1. Nay, sometimes when Sinners have been in the height of their Resistance and Rebellion, to shew the exceeding Riches of his Grace, God has then Converted them. Thus it was with *Saul* afterwards *Paul*, when he was breathing out Slaughters against the Disciples of the Lord, then did God give him Faith in Christ, without his Praying for it. Thus also those Converts in the Second Chapter of the Acts. Not many days before

---

From Increase Mather, *Awakening Truths Tending to Conversion* (Boston, 1710), pp. 66–76; in *The Puritans*, ed. Perry Miller and Thomas H. Johnson (New York: Torchbook eds., Harper & Row, 1963), pp. 335–39.

their Conversion they had been Murdering the Son of God. And just before the Sermon began they were mocking of the Preacher, and yet Converted by that Sermon. Such Instances there have been known in the World, of men that have come to hear a Sermon only to deride it, and yet have been Savingly wrought upon by it. A credible Author reports, that two profane men drinking together, knowing that Mr. *Hooker* was to Preach, one of them said to the other, *Let us go hear how Hooker will baul,* yet was he Converted by that very Sermon, which he went to hear with a Scornful Spirit. And after that had such a love for Mr. *Hooker,* as to remove three thousand Miles, that so he might live under his Ministry. Such Examples are wonderful Evidence of Sovereign Grace.

2. Altho' it is true, (as has been shewed) that Sinners cannot Convert themselves, their *Cannot* is a wilful *Cannot.* Math. 22. 2. *They will not come.* It is not said they *could not* (tho' they could not of themselves come to Christ) but that they *would not* come. If it were in the power of a Sinner to Convert himself, he would not do it: For he hates Conversion. *It is abomination to fools to depart from evil,* Prov. 13. 19. Psal. 50. 17. *Thou hatest instruction.* If they hate to be Converted they will not chuse it. Prov. 1. 29. *They hated knowledge, and did not chuse the fear of the Lord.* Their hearts are in Love, and in League with their Lusts, yea they hate to be *turned* from them: They love darkness rather than light, they hate the light, neither come they to the light, *Joh.* 3. 19, 20. Sinners are haters of God: they say and think that they love him, but the Lord knows that they hate him, and therefore they will not repent of their Sins, and believe on Christ. Christ said to the Jews, *You will not come to me that you might have Life,* Joh. 5. 40. No, they would dy first. And why would they not come? The reason of their Aversion is mentioned in v. 42. *I know you, that you have not the Love of God in you.* Their carnal unregenerate Minds were full of enmity against God, and therefore they would not come to Jesus Christ the Son of God. They cannot Convert themselves, and they are not willing that God should Convert them. If Sinners were willing to have Grace and Holiness, why do they not repair to him for it, who alone can give it to them? An hungry man is willing to have bread, therefore he will seek after it, where ever it is to be had. When the Egyptians were hunger bitten, they went to Pharoah, crying for bread, he bid them go to Joseph, and they did so. Thus if Sinners were willing to be Converted, they would cry

to God to turn them: whenas there are many Sinners that did never put up one earnest Prayer to God in their Lives, that he would bestow Converting Grace on them.

3. Sinners can do more towards their own Conversion than they do or will do. They should give *diligence* to make sure of their being effectually called. They should *strive* to enter in at the strait gate. Conversion is the strait gate that leadeth unto Salvation. They should *Labour* not for the meat that perisheth, but for that which endureth to Everlasting Life: but they do not give diligence, they do not strive, they do not labour to obtain Grace and Salvation: Therefore they perish, and perish justly. Prov. 21. 25. *The desire of the slothful kills him, for his hands refuse to labour.* Men say that they desire Grace, and yet their hands refuse to Labour, they will be at no pains to obtain it: And this slothfulness kills them. It proves the death of their Souls. *The Soul of the sluggard desireth and has nothing, but the Soul of the diligent shall be made fat,* Prov. 13. 4. There are several things which Sinners have power to do in order to their own Conversion, & which they ought to do, but they will not.

(1) They have power to avoid those things which are an hindrance of Conversion. *e.g.* They can if they will forbear the outward Acts of sin. By giving way to sin their hearts are hardned, and their Conversion becomes the more difficult. Heb. 3. 13. *Take heed lest any of you be hardned through the deceitfulness of sin.* But Sinners give way to many sins which they could abstain from, if they would. A Sabbath-breaker can forbear his profaning of the Sabbath. An ungodly Swearer can forbear his profane Oathes, if he will. A Lyar can forbear telling such Lyes. Sinners can avoid the Temptations which will endanger their falling into sin. He that knows that if he goeth to such a place, or into such a company, he will probably be drawn into sin, ought to avoid the Temptation. Prov. 4. 14. *Avoid it, turn from it, and pass away.* The Sinner can do so if he will, but he will not keep out of the way of Temptation. A drunkard will not avoid the Temptation to that his sin. Prov. 23. 31. *Look not on the Wine when it giveth his colour.* He can chuse whether he will look on the wine or no: he has power to refrain, but will not. Thus men by habituating themselves to sin, do what in them is to hinder their own Conversion. Jer. 13. 23. *Can the Ethiopian change his skin, or the Leopard his Spots? then may you also do good that are accustomed to do evil.* Again, Evil Com-

panions hinder Conversion. *Alas! Alas! Alas!* these have been the Eternal ruin of many a Young Man, that was in an hopeful way for Conversion: He has fallen in with vain Companions, they have given him bad Counsel, so have Convictions been stifled, and the motions of Gods holy Spirit quenched in his Soul. The word of the Lord sayes, *Forsake the foolish & Live*, Prov. 9. 6. The Sinner has power to forsake them, but he will not tho' he dies for it.

(2) Sinners have power to wait on God in the use of means which has a tendency to promote Conversion. They can if they will, not only forsake evil Companions, but associate themselves with those that are good: Then are they in the way of Conversion. Prov. 13. 20. *He that walketh with wise men shall be wise, but a Companion of fools shall be destroyed.* That Learned & Holy Man Dr. *Goodwin* in the account which he giveth of his Conversion, declares, That when he was a Young Schollar in the University of *Cambridge*, there were in that *College*, which he belonged unto, a *Number of holy Youth's* (that's his Expression) his associating himself with them was an happy means of furthering the work of Conversion in his Soul. This Unconverted Sinners have power to do. Their feet are as able to carry them to a godly Meeting as to an ungodly one. Reading the Scripture has sometimes been the Means of Conversion. I could tell you of several Learned Jews that were Converted from their Judaism by Reading the 53. Chapter of Isaiah. The famous Fr. *Junius*, was Converted from his *Atheism* by reading the first Chapter of John's Gospel. He that can read is able to read the Scripture, and Books which promote Godliness in the power of it, but a Sinful Creature chuseth rather to mispend his Time in reading vain Romances, or it may be worse Books. A diligent attendence to the Word of God is the way to obtain Converting Grace. Rom. 10. 17. *Faith comes by hearing, and hearing by the Word of God.* Sinners many Times do not mind what they hear. Nay, it may be they will *Set themselves to sleep when God is speaking to them* by his Minister? And shall they then complain, that they cannot Convert themselves, & that God will not Convert them? Once more, Serious thinking & Consideration on Spiritual and Eternal things is oftentimes blessed unto Conversion. This is what God has given men power to do, if they will use that power. They ought seriously to think what they have done, and what they are, and what their end is like to be. If they would do so, it may be Repentance would be the effect of it. . . .

Chapter II

Isaac Newton (1642-1727)

The Renaissance not only sparked the Reformation's challenge to medieval religion but also stimulated a reevaluation of scientific assumptions. The medieval scientist adhered to a Ptolemaic or Aristotelian concept of a motionless earth around which the heavenly bodies revolved. By the end of the sixteenth century, however, more accurate observations of the motions of heavenly bodies made it increasingly difficult to accept the Ptolemaic system. In 1543 Nicholas Copernicus, a Polish-German astronomer, revived the suggestion of a heliocentric universe which the Middle Ages had discarded. Copernicus' contemporaries did not immediately accept his theory, partly because it received the Church's disapproval and partly because he could not offer the theoretical formulations necessary to support it. How could a body such as the earth (much less the other planets and stars) remain in constant motion? There were, at that time, no accepted laws of motion which could answer this question.

Yet within the European scientific community were those who found substance in Copernicus' theory. Among them was the Italian astronomer Galileo Galilei (1564–1642), who spent his life attacking the objections to the Copernican system and eventually arrived at a formulation of the law of inertia: bodies once set in motion will remain in motion until another force brings them to rest. Galileo, like Copernicus, fell under the displeasure of ecclesiastical authorities, but his work attracted attention throughout Europe and ushered in the scientific revolution of the seventeenth century.

Much of the scientific revolution rested upon mathematical demonstration, because it was difficult to devise experiments which duplicated the actions of heavenly bodies. In his *Discourse on Method* (1637) the French philosopher and scientist René Descartes (1596–1650) argued for the application of a mathematical approach to all sciences. Descartes' precise explanation of his ideas enhanced his popularity at the expense of his competitor Sir Francis Bacon (1561–1626), who advocated more empirical demonstrations. Not until the end of the century would two Englishmen, John Locke and Isaac Newton, undercut the Frenchman's sway and prove some of his conclusions wrong.

In 1665, while on an enforced vacation because the plague had closed his college, Isaac Newton began working on the concept of universal gravitation which would resolve the difficulties of the Copernican system by explaining how large bodies, such as planets, could remain in place while revolving about the sun. Twenty-two years later, in 1687, he published his findings in the *Mathematical Principles of Natural Philosophy*.

In methodology Newton bridged the gap between Bacon and Descartes by combining mathematical proof with observations. The *Principles* was a judicious summary of all that had gone before as well as of Newton's own work, presenting a universe which was orderly, static, and harmonious because unchangeable natural laws governed all its operations.

The implications not merely for science but for religion were profound, for Newton's universe no longer nestled so closely in the hand of God. Although Newton sought to avoid theological discussions, those who read him drew their own conclusions. When he died in 1727 his book was well on the way to working a revolution in religion comparable in its implications to the scientific revolution which it had completed.

The selection which follows is the "General Scholium" or summation which Newton added to the original text in 1713. The "hypothesis of vortices" refers to the Cartesian explanation for the motions of the planets, an explanation which Newton was refuting.

Isaac Newton:
Mathematical Principles of Natural Philosophy (1713)

General Scholium

. . . The motions of the comets are exceedingly regular, are governed by the same laws with the motions of the planets, and can by no means be accounted for by the hypothesis of vortices; for comets are carried with very eccentric motions through all parts of the heavens indifferently, with a freedom that is incompatible with the notion of a vortex.

Bodies projected in our air suffer no resistance but from the air. Withdraw the air, as is done in Mr. *Boyle's* vacuum, and the resistance ceases; for in this void a bit of fine down and a piece of solid gold descend with equal velocity. And the same argument must apply to the celestial spaces above the earth's atmosphere; in these spaces, where there is no air to resist their motions, all bodies will move with the greatest freedom; and the planets and comets will constantly pursue their revolutions in orbits given in kind and position, according to the laws above explained; but though these bodies may, indeed, continue in their orbits by the mere laws of gravity, yet they could by no means have at first derived the regular position of the orbits themselves from those laws.

The six primary planets are revolved about the sun in circles concentric with the sun, and with motions directed towards the same parts, and almost in the same plane. Ten moons are revolved about the earth, Jupiter, and Saturn, in circles concentric with them, with the same direction of motion, and nearly in the planes of the orbits of those planets; but it is not to be conceived that mere mechanical causes could give birth to so many regular motions, since the comets range over all parts of the heavens in very eccentric orbits; for by that kind of motion they pass easily through the orbs of the planets, and with great rapidity; and in their aphelions, where they move the slowest, and are detained the longest, they recede to the greatest distances from each other, and hence suffer the least disturbance from their mutual attractions. This

From Sir Isaac Newton, *The Mathematical Principles of Natural Philosophy*, trans. Andrew Motte, 3 vols. (London: Printed for H. D. Symonds, 1803), vol. II, pp. 310–14.

most beautiful system of the sun, planets, and comets, could only proceed from the counsel and dominion of an intelligent and powerful Being. And if the fixed stars are the centres of other like systems, these, being formed by the like wise counsel, must be all subject to the dominion of One; especially since the light of the fixed stars is of the same nature with the light of the sun, and from every system light passes into all the other systems: and lest the systems of the fixed stars should, by their gravity, fall on each other, he hath placed those systems at immense distances from one another.

This Being governs all things, not as the soul of the world, but as Lord over all; and on account of his dominion he is wont to be called *Lord God* παντοκράτωρ, or *Universal Ruler;* for *God* is a relative word, and has a respect to servants; and *Deity* is the dominion of God not over his own body, as those imagine who fancy God to be the soul of the world, but over servants. The Supreme God is a Being eternal, infinite, absolutely perfect; but a being, however perfect, without dominion, cannot be said to be Lord God; for we say, my God, your God, the God of *Israel*, the God of Gods, and Lord of Lords; but we do not say, my Eternal, your Eternal, the Eternal of *Israel*, the Eternal of Gods; we do not say, my Infinite, or my Perfect: these are titles which have no respect to servants. The word God usually signifies *Lord;* but every lord is not a God. It is the dominion of a spiritual being which constitutes a God: a true, supreme, or imaginary dominion makes a true, supreme, or imaginary God. And from his true dominion it follows that the true God is a living, intelligent, and powerful Being; and, from his other perfections, that he is supreme, or most perfect. He is eternal and infinite, omnipotent and omniscient; that is, his duration reaches from eternity to eternity; his presence from infinity to infinity; he governs all things, and knows all things that are or can be done. He is not eternity and infinity, but eternal and infinite; he is not duration or space, but he endures and is present. He endures forever, and is everywhere present; and, by existing always and everywhere, he constitutes duration and space. Since every particle of space is *always*, and every indivisible moment of duration is *everywhere*, certainly the Maker and Lord of all things cannot be *never* and *nowhere*. Every soul that has perception is, though in different times and in different organs of sense and motion, still the same indivisible person. There are given successive

parts in duration, coexistent parts in space, but neither the one nor
the other in the person of a man, or his thinking principle; and
much less can they be found in the thinking substance of God.
Every man, so far as he is a thing that has perception, is one and
the same man during his whole life, in all and each of his organs
of sense. God is the same God, always and everywhere. He is
omnipresent not *virtually* only, but also *substantially;* for virtue
cannot subsist without substance. In him are all things contained
and moved; yet neither affects the other: God suffers nothing from
the motion of bodies; bodies find no resistance from the omnipres-
ence of God. It is allowed by all that the Supreme God exists necessarily; and by the same necessity he exists *always* and *everywhere.*
Whence also he is all similar, all eye, all ear, all brain, all arm, all
power to perceive, to understand, and to act; but in a manner not
at all human, in a manner not at all corporeal, in a manner utterly
unknown to us. As a blind man has no idea of colors, so have we
no idea of the manner by which the all-wise God perceives and
understands all things. He is utterly void of all body and bodily
figure, and can therefore neither be seen, nor heard, nor touched;
nor ought he to be worshipped under the representation of any
corporeal thing. We have ideas of his attributes, but what the real
substance of anything is we know not. In bodies, we see only their
figures and colors, we hear only the sounds, we touch only their
outward surfaces, we smell only the smells, and taste the savors;
but their inward substances are not to be known either by our
senses, or by any reflex act of our minds: much less, then, have
we any idea of the substance of God. We know him only by his
most wise and excellent contrivances of things, and final causes;
we admire him for his perfections; but we reverence and adore
him on account of his dominion: for we adore him as his servants;
and a god without dominion, providence, and final causes, is
nothing else but Fate and Nature. Blind metaphysical necessity,
which is certainly the same always and everywhere, could produce
no variety of things. All that diversity of natural things which we
find suited to different times and places could rise from nothing
but the ideas and will of a being necessarily existing. But, by way
of allegory, God is said to see, to speak, to laugh, to love, to hate,
to desire, to give, to receive, to rejoice, to be angry, to fight, to
frame, to work, to build; for all our notions of God are taken from
the ways of mankind by a certain similitude, which, though not

perfect, has some likeness, however. And thus much concerning God; to discourse of whom from the appearances of things, does certainly belong to Natural Philosophy.

Cotton Mather: The Christian Philosopher (1721)

By the latter part of the eighteenth century, the concept of a universe controlled by mechanical laws working inevitably and unalterably, always in the same way for all time—the so-called Newtonian world-view—infused all facets of American thought. Commonplace are such comparisons as Jefferson makes when he writes,

> I dare say that in time all these [states] as well as their central government, like the planets revolving around their common sun, acting and acted upon according to their respective weights and distances, will produce that beautiful equilibrium on which our Constitution is founded, and which I believe it will exhibit to the world in a degree of perfection, unexampled but in the planetary system itself.

The first copy of Newton's *Principles* known to be in America was donated to the Yale library in 1726, but even before that time, such men as the noted Puritan divine Cotton Mather (1662–1727) were spreading Newton's ideas. In *The Christian Philosopher* (1721) Mather sought to show that Newton's findings reaffirmed the traditional doctrines of Christianity.

Newton's other popularizers included Benjamin Franklin, whose *Poor Richard's Almanac* carried articles on modern astronomy along with its advice to farmers on when to plant crops, and Nathaniel Ames, who also included descriptions of the Newtonian solar system in his widely read almanacs.

A number of other eighteenth-century Americans were thoroughly familiar with Isaac Newton's work. Cadwallader Colden, lieutenant governor of New York, physician, anthropologist, botanist, physicist, and mathematician, published a critique of Newtonian physics, *An Explanation of the First Causes of Action in Matter, and of the Cause of Gravitation* (1745). James Logan, a Philadelphia merchant and agent for the Penn family, mastered Newton's Principles, as did another Philadelphian, David Rittenhouse, who made some significant if not spectacular contributions to astronomy and obtained international fame when he constructed a teaching machine in 1767. This machine, the Rittenhouse Orrery, simulated the motions of the planets and their satellites, at any point in time backward or forward for 5,000 years, thus providing students and spectators with a mechanical representation of the Newtonian system.

The following selection from Cotton Mather's *Christian Philosopher* draws directly from Newton's discussion of comets, and also includes an argument for the existence of God based upon the design evidenced in nature—an argument very similar to Newton's. In addition, Mather used several works in the realm of natural theology, such as William C. Cheyne's *Philosophical Principles of Natural Religion* (1705) and William Derham's *Astro-Theology* (1715). Both Cheyne and Derham attempted to support religious doctrine with arguments drawn from natural science.

Of Comets

'Tis an admirable Work of our GOD, that the many *Globes* in the Universe are placed at such Distances, as to avoid all violent Shocks upon one another, and every thing wherein they might prove a prejudice to one another.

Even *Comets* too, move so as to serve the Holy Ends of their Creator! Comets, which are commonly called *Blazing Stars*, appear unto later Observations to be a sort of *Excentrical Planets*, that move periodically about the *Sun*.

Sir *Isaac Newton*, from whom 'tis a difficult thing to dissent in any thing that belongs to *Philosophy*, concludes, That the Bodies of *Comets* are solid, compact, fixed, and durable, even like those of the other *Planets*.

He has a very critical Thought upon the *Heat*, which these *Bodies* may suffer in their Transits near the Sun. A famous one, in the Year 1680, passed so near the *Sun*, that the *Heat* of the *Sun* in it must be twenty-eight thousand times as intense as it is in *England* at Midsummer; whereas the Heat of boiling Water, as he tried, is but little more than the dry Earth of that Island, exposed unto the Midsummer-Sun: and the *Heat* of *red-hot Iron* he takes to be three or four times as great as that of *boiling Water*. Wherefore

From Cotton Mather, *The Christian Philosopher* (London: Emanuel Matthews, 1721), pp. 41–45.

the *Heat* of that *Comet* in its *Perihelion* was near two thousand times as great as that of *red-hot Iron*. If it had been an Aggregate of nothing but Exhalations, the *Sun* would have render'd it invisible. A Globe of *red-hot Iron*, of the Dimensions of our Earth, would scarce be cool, by his Computation, in 50,000 Years. If then this *Comet* cooled an hundred times as fast as *red-hot Iron*, yet, since his Heat was 2,000 times greater than that of *red-hot Iron*, if you suppose his Body no greater than that of this Earth, he will not be cool in a Million of Years.

The *Tails* of *Comets*, which are longest and largest just after their *Perihelions*, he takes to be a long and very thin Smoke, or a mighty Train of Vapours, which the ignited *Nucleus*, or the Head of the *Comet*, emits from it. And he easily and thoroughly confounds the silly Notion of their being only the *Beams of the Sun*, shining thro the Head of the *Star*.

The Phaenomena of the *Tails of Comets* depend upon the Motion of their *Heads*, and have their Matter supplied from thence.

There may arise from the Atmosphere of *Comets*, Vapours enough to take up such immense Spaces, as we see they do. Computations made of and from the Rarity of our *Air*, which by and by issue in Astonishments, will render this Matter evident.

That the Tails of *Comets* are extremely rare, is apparent from this; the *Fixed Stars* appearing so plainly thro them.

The Atmosphere of *Comets*, as they descend towards the *Sun*, is very sensibly diminished by their vast running out, that they may afford Matter to produce the *Blaze*. *Hevelius* has observed, that their Atmosphere is enlarged, when they do not so much run out into *Tail*.

This *Lucid Train* sometimes, as Dr. *Cheyne* observes, extends to four hundred thousand Miles above the Body of the *Star*.

Sir *Isaac Newton* has an Apprehension, which is a little surprizing, That those Vapours which are dilated, and go off in the Blazes of *Comets*, and are diffused thro all the Celestial Regions, may by little and little, by their own proper *Gravity*, be attracted into the *Planets*, and become intermingled with their Atmospheres. As to the Constitution of such an *Earth* as ours, it is necessary there should be *Seas;* thus, for the Conservation of the *Seas*, and Moisture of the Planets, there may be a necessity of *Comets;* from whose condensed Vapours, all that *Moisture*, which is consumed in Vegetations and Putrefactions, and so turned into dry Earth, may by degrees be continually supplied, repaired, and recruited. Yea, he has a suspicion, that the Spirit, which is the finest, the most subtile, and the very best part of our *Air*, and which is necessarily requisite unto the Life and Being of all things, comes chiefly from *Comets*. If this be so, the Appearance of *Comets* is not so dreadful a thing, as the *Cometomantia*, generally prevailing, has represented it.

Mr. *Cassini* will thus far allow bad Presages to *Comets*, That if the Tail of a *Comet* should be too much intermingled with our *Atmosphere*, or if the Matter of it should, by its *Gravity*, fall down upon our Earth; it may induce those Changes in our *Air*, whereof we should be very sensible.

Bernoulli, in his *Systema Cometarum*, supposes, That there is a *Primary Planet*, revolving round the *Sun* in the space of four Years and 157 Days; and at the distance of 2,583 Semidiameters of the *Orbis Magnus*. This *Primary Planet*, he supposes, either from his mighty *Distance*, or his minute *Smallness*, to be not visible unto us; but however to have several *Satellits* moving round him, tho none descending so low as the Orbit of *Saturn;* and that these becoming visible to us, when in their *Perigaon*, are what we call *Comets*.

Seneca's Prediction, That a Time should come, when our Mysteries of *Comets* should be unfolded, seems almost accomplished. However *Seneca* has not obliged us with the *Phanomena* observed by him, which encouraged this Prediction.

No Histories of *Comets* were of service to the Theory of them, until *Nicephirus Gregoras*, a *Constantinopolitan* Astronomer, described the Path of a Comet in 1337.

All that consider'd *Comets* until *Tycho Brahe*, consider'd them as no other than Vapours below the *Moon*.

Anon, the sagacious *Kepler* improving on *Tycho's* Discoveries, came at a true System of *Comets*, and found, that they moved freely through the Planetary Orbs, with a Motion that is not much different from a *Rectilinear* one.

The incomparable *Hevelius* went on, and though he embraced the *Keplerian* Hypothesis, of the *Rectilinear Motion of Comets*, yet he was aware, *That the Path of a Comet was bent into a curve Line towards the Sun.*

At last the illustrious Sir *Isaac Newton* arrives with Demonstrations, That all the Phaenomena of *Comets* would naturally follow from the *Keplerian* Principles. He shewed a Method of delineating the *Orbits* of *Comets* geometrically; which caused Admiration in all that considered it, and comprehended it.

The most ingenious Dr. *Halley* has made Calculations, upon which he ventures to foretell the *Return* of *Comets;* but he observes, that some of them have their *Nodes* pretty near the annual Orb of the Earth. I will transcribe the Words he concludes with: 'What may be the *Consequences* of so near an Appulse, or of a *Contact,* or lastly, of a *Shock* of the Celestial Bodies (which is by no means impossible to come to pass) I leave to be discussed by the Studious of Physical Matters.'

The Sentiments of so acute a Philosopher as Dr. *Cheyne* upon *Comets,* deserve to be transcribed.

'I think it most probable, that these frightful Bodies are the Ministers of *Divine Justice,* and in their Visits lend us *benign* or *noxious* Vapours, according to the Designs of Providence; That they may have brought, and may still bring about the great Catastrophe of our System; and, That they may be the Habitation of *Animals* in a State of *Punishment,* which if it did not look too notional, there are many Arguments to render not improbable.'

And elsewhere: ' 'Tis most likely, they are the Ministers of Divine Justice, sending baneful Steams, from their long Trains, upon the *Planets* they come nigh. However, from them we may learn that the Divine Vengeance may find a *Seat* for the *Punishment* of his disobedient Creatures, without being put to the expence of a New Creation.'

When I see a vast Comet, blazing and rolling about the unmeasurable *Æther,* I will think;

'Who can tell, but I now see a wicked World *made a fiery Oven in the Time of the Anger of GOD! The Lord swallowing them up in his Wrath, and the Fire devouring them!*

'What prodigious Mischief and Ruin might such a *Ball of Confusion* bring upon our sinful *Globe,* if the Great GOD order its Approach to us!

'How happy they, that are in the Favour and Friendship of that Glorious Lord, who *knows how to deliver the Pious* out of Distresses, and *reserve the Unjust for a Punishment of a Day of Judgment!'*

Chapter III

John Locke (1632-1704)

Just as Newton undermined some (but by no means all) of Descartes's scientific contributions, so another Englishman, John Locke, succeeded in destroying a part of Descartes's authority in the realm of philosophy. Descartes had argued that there were some ideas so clearly manifest to the mind that it accepted them *a priori*. His followers interpreted this somewhat carelessly to mean that the mind contained innate ideas; this became the epistemological theory of the seventeenth century.

While Locke was a student at Oxford, his study of Descartes generated an interest in philosophy. His first vocations, however, were medicine and science; after receiving a B.A. in 1652 and an M.A. in 1658, he remained at Oxford teaching Greek and rhetoric and pursuing scientific studies.

One of Locke's friends was Anthony Ashley Cooper, later the first earl of Shaftesbury. First as physician and then as family counselor, Locke took up residence in his friend's home. Shaftesbury was a political schemer, however, whose activities aimed at preventing a restoration of Catholicism earned him the enmity of both Charles II and James II. Though his friend's machinations do not seem to have involved Locke, he nevertheless incurred the suspicion of the government and fled to Holland in 1683. His sojourn in Holland brought him into touch with the Dutch court of William and Mary. In February of 1689, after the expulsion of James II and the victory of William, Locke returned to England on the same ship as the Princess Mary.

Locke's reputation as a philosopher rests upon the famous *Essay Concerning Human Understanding*. In 1670 a discussion with a few friends led him to a consideration of the limits of human knowledge. Thinking to set down on one sheet of paper his whole theory of epistemology, he began work upon the essay which was to stand as an authoritative statement until Immanuel Kant. By 1679 he spoke of it as finished, but not until 1690 did a complete version appear in print. By the end of the eighteenth century there were some twenty different editions of the "essay." Its impact was tremendous, for, in asserting that man's knowledge came to him from his environment, Locke opened the way for the characteristic eighteenth-century belief in environmentalism—the position that man was the product of his environment. Human nature seemed to be malleable; in shaping his environment, man could shape himself and produce a utopia without war, crime, or insanity. Locke created a revolution in man's appreciation of his own potential.

Essay Concerning Human Understanding (1690)

No Innate Principles in the Mind

2. There is nothing more commonly taken for granted, than that there are certain principles, both speculative and practical (for they speak of both), universally agreed upon by all mankind; which therefore, they argue, must needs be constant impressions, which the souls of men receive in their first beings, and which they bring into the world with them as necessarily and really as they do any of their inherent faculties.

3. This argument, drawn from universal consent, has this misfortune in it; that if it were true in matter of fact, that there were certain truths, wherein all mankind agreed, it would not prove them innate, if there can be any other way shown, how men may

---

From John Locke, *Works* (London: Thomas Tegg; W. Sharpe & Son; G. Offor; G. & J. Robinson; J. Evans & Co.; Glasgow: R. Griffin & Co.; Dublin: J. Cummin, 1823).

come to that universal agreement in the things they do consent in;
which I presume may be done.

4. But, which is worse, this argument of universal consent,
which is made use of to prove innate principles, seems to me a
demonstration that there are none such; because there are none
to which all mankind give an universal assent. I shall begin with
the speculative, and instance in those magnified principles of
demonstration; "whatsoever is, is;" and, "it is impossible for the
same thing to be, and not to be;" which, of all others, I think have
the most allowed title to innate. These have so settled a reputation
of maxims universally received, that it will, no doubt, be thought
strange, if any one should seem to question it. But yet I take liberty
to say, that these propositions are so far from having an universal
assent, that there are great part of mankind to whom they are not
so much as known.

5. For, first, it is evident, that all children and idiots have not
the least apprehension or thought of them; and the want of that is
enough to destroy that universal assent, which must needs be the
necessary concomitant of all innate truths: it seeming to me near
a contradiction, to say, that there are truths imprinted on the soul,
which it perceives or understands not; imprinting, if it signify any
thing, being nothing else, but the making certain truths to be perceived. For to imprint any thing on the mind, without the mind's
perceiving it, seems to me hardly intelligible. If therefore children
and idiots have souls, have minds, with those impressions upon
them, they must unavoidably perceive them, and necessarily know
and assent to these truths; which, since they do not, it is evident
that there are no such impressions: for if they are not notions naturally imprinted, how can they be innate? and if they are notions
imprinted, how can they be unknown? To say a notion is imprinted
on the mind, and yet at the same time to say, that the mind is
ignorant of it, and never yet took notice of it, is to make this impression nothing. No proposition can be said to be in the mind,
which it never yet knew, which it was never yet conscious of: for if
any one may, then, by the same reason, all propositions that are
true, and the mind is capable of ever assenting to, may be said to
be in the mind, and to be imprinted: since, if any one can be said
to be in the mind, which it never yet knew, it must be only, because
it is capable of knowing it; and so the mind is of all truths it ever

shall know. Nay, thus truths may be imprinted on the mind, which it never did, nor ever shall know: for a man may live long, and die at last in ignorance of many truths, which his mind was capable of knowing, and that with certainty. So that if the capacity of knowing be the natural impression contended for, all the truths a man ever comes to know, will, by this account, be every one of them innate; and this great point will amount to no more, but only to a very improper way of speaking; which, whilst it pretends to assert the contrary, says nothing different from those who deny innate principles: for nobody, I think, ever denied that the mind was capable of knowing several truths. The capacity, they say, is innate, the knowledge acquired. But then to what end such contest for certain innate maxims? If truths can be imprinted on the understanding without being perceived, I can see no difference there can be between any truths the mind is capable of knowing, in respect of their original: they must all be innate, or all adventitious: in vain shall a man go about to distinguish them. He, therefore, that talks of innate notions in the understanding, cannot (if he intend thereby any distinct sort of truths) mean such truths to be in the understanding, as it never perceived, and is yet wholly ignorant of: for if these words (to be in the understanding) have any propriety, they signify to be understood: so that, to be in the understanding, and not to be understood—to be in the mind, and never to be perceived—is all one, as to say, any thing is, and is not, in the mind or understanding. If therefore these two propositions, "whatsoever is, is," and "it is impossible for the same thing to be, and not to be," are by nature imprinted, children cannot be ignorant of them; infants, and all that have souls, must necessarily have them in their understandings, know the truth of them, and assent to it.

6. To avoid this, it is usually answered, That all men know and assent to them, when they come to the use of reason, and this is enough to prove them innate. I answer,

7. Doubtful expressions, that have scarce any signification, go for clear reasons to those, who being prepossessed, take not the pains to examine even what they themselves say. For to apply this answer with any tolerable sense to our present purpose, it must signify one of these two things: either, that, as soon as men come to the use of reason, these supposed native inscriptions come to be

known and observed by them; or else, that the use and exercise of men's reason assists them in the discovery of these principles, and certainly makes them known to them.

8. If they mean, that by the use of reason men may discover these principles, and that this is sufficient to prove them innate; their way of arguing will stand thus: viz. that whatever truths reason can certainly discover to us, and make us firmly assent to, those are all naturally imprinted on the mind; since that universal assent, which is made the mark of them, amounts to no more but this; that by the use of reason we are capable to come to a certain knowledge of, and assent to them; and, by this means, there will be no difference between the maxims of the mathematicians, and theorems they deduce from them: all must be equally allowed innate; they being all discoveries made by the use of reason, and truths that a rational creature may certainly come to know, if he apply his thoughts rightly that way.

9. But how can these men think the use of reason necessary to discover principles that are supposed innate, when reason (if we may believe them) is nothing else but the faculty of deducing unknown truths from principles, or propositions, that are already known? That certainly can never be thought innate, which we have need of reason to discover; unless, as I have said, we will have all the certain truths that reason ever teaches us, to be innate. We may as well think the use of reason necessary to make our eyes discover visible objects, as that there should be need of reason, or the exercise thereof, to make the understanding see what is originally engraven on it, and cannot be in the understanding before it be perceived by it. So that to make reason discover those truths thus imprinted, is to say, that the use of reason discovers to a man what he knew before; and if men have those innate impressed truths originally, and before the use of reason, and yet are always ignorant of them, till they come to the use of reason; it is in effect to say, that men know, and know them not, at the same time.

No Innate Practical Principles

1. If those speculative maxims, whereof we discoursed in the foregoing chapter, have not an actual universal assent from all mankind, as we there proved, it is much more visible concerning practical principles, that they come short of an universal reception: and

I think it will be hard to instance any one moral rule which can pretend to so general and ready an assent as, "what is, is"; or to be so manifest a truth as this, "that it is impossible for the same thing to be, and not to be." Whereby it is evident, that they are farther removed from a title to be innate; and the doubt of their being native impressions on the mind is stronger against those moral principles than the other. Not that it brings their truth at all in question: they are equally true, though not equally evident. Those speculative maxims carry their own evidence with them; but moral principles require reasoning and discourse, and some exercise of the mind, to discover the certainty of their truth. They lie not open as natural characters engraven on the mind; which, if any such were, they must needs be visible by themselves, and by their own light be certain and known to every body. But this is no derogation to their truth and certainty, no more than it is to the truth or certainty of the three angles of a triangle being equal to two right ones; because it is not so evident, as "the whole is bigger than a part;" nor so apt to be assented to at first hearing. It may suffice, that these moral rules are capable of demonstration; and therefore it is our own fault if we come not to a certain knowledge of them. But the ignorance wherein many men are of them, and the slowness of assent wherewith others receive them, are manifest proofs that they are not innate, and such as offer themselves to their view without searching.

2. Whether there be any such moral principles, wherein all men do agree, I appeal to any, who have been but moderately conversant in the history of mankind, and looked abroad beyond the smoke of their own chimneys. Where is that practical truth, that is universally received without doubt or question, as it must be, if innate? Justice, and keeping of contracts, is that which most men seem to agree in. This is a principle which is thought to extend itself to the dens of thieves, and the confederacies of the greatest villains; and they who have gone farthest towards the putting off of humanity itself, keep faith and rules of justice one with another. I grant that outlaws themselves do this one amongst another; but it is without receiving these as the innate laws of nature. They practise them as rules of convenience within their own communities: but it is impossible to conceive, that he embraces justice as a practical principle, who acts fairly with his fellow-highwayman, and at the same time plunders or kills the next honest man he

meets with. Justice and truth are the common ties of society; and, therefore, even outlaws and robbers, who break with all the world besides, must keep faith and rules of equity amongst themselves, or else they cannot hold together. But will any one say, that those that live by fraud or rapine have innate principles of truth and justice which they allow and assent to?

3. Perhaps it will be urged, that the tacit assent of their minds agrees to what their practice contradicts. I answer, first, I have always thought the actions of men the best interpreters of their thoughts. But since it is certain, that most men's practices, and some men's open professions, have either questioned or denied these principles, it is impossible to establish an universal consent (though we should look for it only amongst grown men), without which it is impossible to conclude them innate. Secondly, it is very strange and unreasonable, to suppose innate practical principles that terminate only in contemplation. Practical principles derived from nature are there for operation, and must produce conformity of action, not barely speculative assent to their truth, or else they are in vain distinguished from speculative maxims. Nature, I confess, has put into man a desire of happiness, and an aversion to misery: these indeed are innate practical principles, which (as practical principles ought) do continue constantly to operate and influence all our actions without ceasing: these may be observed, in all persons and all ages, steady and universal; but these are inclinations of the appetite to good, not impressions of truth on the understanding. I deny not that there are natural tendencies imprinted on the minds of men; and that, from the very first instances of sense and perception, there are some things that are grateful, and others unwelcome to them; some things that they incline to, and others that they fly: but this makes nothing for innate characters on the mind, which are to be the principles of knowledge, regulating our practice. Such natural impressions on the understanding are so far from being confirmed hereby, that this is an argument against them; since, if there were certain characters imprinted by nature on the understanding, as the principles of knowledge, we could not but perceive them constantly operate in us, and influence our knowledge, as we do those others on the will and appetite; which never cease to be the constant springs and motives of all our actions, to which we perpetually feel them strongly impelling us.

4. Another reason that makes me doubt of any innate practical principles, is, that I think there cannot any one moral rule be proposed, whereof a man may not justly demand a reason: which would be perfectly ridiculous and absurd, if they were innate, or so much as self-evident; which every innate principle must needs be, and not need any proof to ascertain its truth, nor want any reason to gain it approbation. He would be thought void of common sense, who asked on the one side, or on the other side went to give, a reason, why it is impossible for the same thing to be, and not to be. It carries its own light and evidence with it, and needs no other proof: he that understands the terms, assents to it for its own sake, or else nothing will ever be able to prevail with him to do it. But should that most unshaken rule of morality, and foundation of all social virtue, "that one should do as he would be done unto," be proposed to one who never heard it before, but yet is of capacity to understand its meaning, might he not without any absurdity ask a reason why? And were not he that proposed it bound to make out the truth and reasonableness of it to him? which plainly shows it not to be innate; for if it were, it could neither want nor receive any proof, but must needs (at least, as soon as heard and understood) be received and assented to as an unquestionable truth, which a man can by no means doubt of. So that the truth of all these moral rules plainly depends upon some other antecedent to them, and from which they must be deduced; which could not be, if either they were innate, or so much as self-evident.

Of Ideas in General, and Their Original

1. Every man being conscious to himself that he thinks, and that which his mind is applied about, whilst thinking, being the ideas that are there, it is past doubt, that men have in their minds several ideas, such as are those expressed by the words whiteness, hardness, sweetness, thinking, motion, man, elephant, army, drunkenness, and others. It is in the first place then to be inquired, how he comes by them. I know it is a received doctrine, that men have native ideas and original characters stamped upon their minds in their very first being. This opinion I have, at large, examined already; and, I suppose, what I have said, in the foregoing book, will be much more easily admitted, when I have shown whence the

understanding may get all the ideas it has, and by what ways and degrees they may come into the mind; for which I shall appeal to every one's own observation and experience.

2. Let us then suppose the mind to be, as we say, white paper, void of all characters, without any ideas; how comes it to be furnished? Whence comes it by that vast store which the busy and boundless fancy of man has painted on it, with an almost endless variety? Whence has it all the materials of reason and knowledge? To this I answer, in one word, from experience: in that all our knowledge is founded, and from that it ultimately derives itself. Our observation employed either about external sensible objects, or about the internal operations of our minds, perceived and reflected on by ourselves, is that which supplies our understandings with all the materials of thinking. These two are the fountains of knowledge, from whence all the ideas we have, or can naturally have, do spring.

3. First, Our senses, conversant about particular sensible objects, do convey into the mind several distinct perceptions of things, according to those various ways wherein those objects do affect them: and thus we come by those ideas we have of yellow, white, heat, cold, soft, hard, bitter, sweet, and all those which we call sensible qualities; which when I say the senses convey into the mind, I mean, they from external objects convey into the mind what produces there those perceptions. This great source of most of the ideas we have, depending wholly upon our senses, and derived by them to the understanding, I call *sensation*.

4. Secondly, The other fountain from which experience furnisheth the understanding with ideas, is the perception of the operations of our own mind within us, as it is employed about the ideas it has got; which operations when the soul comes to reflect on and consider, do furnish the understanding with another set of ideas, which could not be had from things without; and such are perception, thinking, doubting, believing, reasoning, knowing, willing, and all the different actings of our own minds; which we being conscious of and observing in ourselves, do from these receive into our understandings as distinct ideas, as we do from bodies affecting our senses. This source of ideas every man has wholly in himself: and though it be not sense, as having nothing to do with external objects, yet it is very like it, and might properly enough be called internal sense. But as I call the other

sensation, so I call this *reflection*, the ideas it affords being such only as the mind gets by reflecting on its own operations within itself. By reflection, then, in the following part of this discourse, I would be understood to mean that notice which the mind takes of its own operations, and the manner of them; by reason whereof there come to be ideas of these operations in the understanding. These two, I say, viz. external material things, as the objects of sensation; and the operations of our own minds within, as the objects of reflection; are to me the only originals from whence all our ideas take their beginnings. The term operations here I use in a large sense, as comprehending not barely the actions of the mind about its ideas, but some sort of passions arising sometimes from them, such as is the satisfaction or uneasiness arising from any thought.

5. The understanding seems to me not to have the least glimmering of any ideas, which it doth not receive from one of these two. External objects furnish the mind with the ideas of sensible qualities, which are all those different perceptions they produce in us: and the mind furnishes the understanding with ideas of its own operations.

These, when we have taken a full survey of them and their several modes, combinations, and relations, we shall find to contain all our whole stock of ideas; and that we have nothing in our minds which did not come in one of these two ways. Let any one examine his own thoughts, and thoroughly search into his understanding; and then let him tell me, whether all the original ideas he has there are any other than of the objects of his senses, or of the operations of his mind, considered as objects of his reflection: and how great a mass of knowledge soever he imagines to be lodged there, he will, upon taking a strict view, see that he has not any idea in his mind, but what one of these two have imprinted; though perhaps with infinite variety compounded and enlarged by the understanding, as we shall see hereafter.

Ethan Allen: Reason, the Only Oracle of Man (1784)

Lockean psychology subtly permeated much of Enlightenment thought in America as well as Europe. One of the earliest examples of Locke's influence in America was the Congregational minister Jonathan Edwards (1703–58). Although better known for his fiery sermons, which contributed to the Great Awakening, Edwards was one of America's greatest philosophers and theologians. He took the ideas of Locke and Newton and incorporated them into a new synthesis with Calvinism.

Although Edwards used Locke's epistemology to buttress orthodoxy, others used it to support more liberal religion. One such work was by the Revolutionary soldier Ethan Allen. Allen completed his *Reason, the Only Oracle of Man* after hostilities had ceased with the British, and published it in 1784. His knowledge of Locke was at least secondhand, acquired from a close friend, Dr. Thomas Young, who attended Yale. Nevertheless, Locke's influence is quite clear in the following selection. (See also page 91.)

Of the Aptitudes of Sensation, and of Their Subserviency to the Mind

The senses are exquisitely well calculated to make discoveries of external objects to the mind, they are the medium through which the mind receives its first notices of things, or mere apprehension of them, without denying or affirming anything concerning them, and it is in, by, or through the instrumentality of the senses only, that the mind of man, in this life, is enabled to form any idea of external objects, or to exert its thinking, conscious nature. The instances of persons born deficient in part, as to their senses, will serve to illustrate the subject matter of our enquiry; those who are born blind, can never be taught what colours are, or what we mean by seeing: an idea of colours, or the knowledge of occular perception, is to them supernatural and impossible; so also respecting those who are born deaf, an idea of sound would to them be equally supernatural; the most harmonious music would to them be as imperceptible, as nonentity is to us, of which they could not form any conception. This we know to be true in fact.

. . .

Whatever external object presents itself to the senses, gives the mind an apprehension of it. To enumerate the diversity and multiplicity of the objects of sense would be endless, and also needless. The notices or apprehensions of things, which are communicated

From Ethan Allen, *Reason, the Only Oracle of Man* (Bennington, Vt.: Haswell & Russell, 1784).

to the mind by the mere aptitude of sensation itself, abstracted from a succession of reflection, or thinking, are what I denominate simple ideas; which are excited by the intervention of the senses between external objects and the mind, and are much the same helps to the mind, as glasses are to the senses, by assisting the natural eye to discover such object, which without them the eye could not perceive, and the mind by that means obtains an apprehension of such extended objects by looking through two mediums, to wit, the eye and the glass, the eye is in this case the first medium, without which the mind could not discern the glass; and the glass the second medium, which enables the eye, and consequently the mind, to discover worlds in the expansion of the heavens, which the mind through its first medium only, could not explore. It is on simple ideas, which the mind thus mediately obtains through the instrumentality of its senses, that all our proficiency in knowledge and science is predicated. There is not one individual apprehension or original simple idea but what the mind receives through its sensory, so that sensation in the order of nature, discloses the way and manner of the exertions of cogitative nature. Common conversation, learning, business and whatever pertains to the social life, is manifestly dependent on it. Those, who are taught the art of reading and writing, can hold correspondence with each other though in different quarters of the globe, by which means we are also enabled to maintain a correspondence of ideas with writers who have been long dead; twenty four characters or letters arranged together, according to certain rules prescribed, are capable of making such an impression on the sense of seeing, that by and through that sense, the mind of those who read can understand the ideas of those who have written intelligibly. "It is not by any concomitant act of raciocination that we come to be apprized of the existence and difference of the common objects of sense; but we find them to be existent and different in and by the pure act of sensation itself; we have in and by this act such a representation of things made to us, that we apprehend, that this is not that, nor one the other. It is true by reason and reflection, we come to a more compleat and particular knowledge of the differences, but we have not our first apprehensions of those differences from thence." Though reason and experience, in a variety of instances, may correct sense; yet independent of it, there could have been no such thing as reasoning or experience among mankind, or any such creature as man, sensation being a part of his nature. There are many modes and customs arbitrarily introduced into learning and arts. It was neither sensation or reason that pointed out any particular shape, sound or name to the twenty-four letters; but it was the effect of contrivance and invention, which are faculties of the mind: nevertheless the mind must have been previously notified, through the medium of its senses, of shapes and sounds in general, or else it had not been able to have conceived of, or to have invented shapes or sounds in particular, which might be adapted to answer the design of communicating or receiving ideas; and thus it is, that sensation in all cases, lays the foundation of the exercise of thought and reflection: judgment is no further concerned in such like cases, than that the figure and size of the letters, and their particular sounds, be uniform and distinct, that the characters might be handily written and printed; and any supposed figure or sound of letters, which are equally well adapted to the design of giving and receiving ideas, and holding intercourse between intelligent beings, are equally approvable by reason, provided they may have obtained common consent and use. The same may be observed of the rules of spelling and many other parts of learning. Language itself is absolutely artificial and arbitrary; for though natural sensation taught all nations to apprehend the common objects of sense alike, yet neither sensation nor reason taught any particular language, and consequently the nations and tribes of the world differ in their speech, though they agree in their sensible apprehensions of external things; but we arbitrarily affix certain ideas to words or sounds, and those, who are acquainted with, and understand their connection, are linguists, and are able to correspond together.

John Locke: Treatises of Civil Government (1690)

Locke's "Essay" had important effects upon subsequent "enlightened" thought, but its subject was a technical matter of most direct interest to those schooled in philosophy. Of far broader popular appeal because of their more "practical" concern were his two "Treatises of Civil Government" (1690).

Modern students frequently tend to think of absolute monarchy as the relic of the Middle Ages. In truth, medieval political theory emphasized a rule of law which limited even the monarch. Absolute monarchy was not a product of feudalism, but rather a reaction against it. Absolutism was the answer to the civil wars generated by the feudal system.

In the seventeenth century, absolutism seemed to many the wave of the future, the tool of reform whereby order could be brought out of the chaos which afflicted many countries. Moreover, it had appeal to intellectuals concerned with seeking rational solutions to the problems of man. Submission to a single unquestioned authority seemed more "rational" than the system of conflicting loyalties imposed by medieval vassalage.

In England the most prominent such intellectual was Thomas Hobbes (1588–1679). Forced to leave England by the outbreak of civil war, Hobbes began his famous work, *Leviathan* (1651), in Paris. Enamored of Descartes's method, Hobbes eschewed historical research; instead he used reason to arrive at what seemed the logical answers. He postulated a "state of nature" in which men lived before the existence of government. Human nature being basically selfish, men in the state of nature were constantly at war with one another; a man's life was "solitary, mean, nasty, brutish, and short." To escape this condition, men met together and entered into a "social contract" to submit to the rule of a sovereign. The parties to this contract were the subjects; it was not a bargain struck with the ruler himself; therefore there were no limits on the sovereign's authority. Since anything was better than the state of nature, the contract was irrevocable. No action by the sovereign could justify breaking the social contract.

However much such a doctrine might appeal to English royalists, it could never receive a favorable hearing among those who sympathized with Parliament's effort to limit the authority of the monarch. Ever since James I (1603–25) had asserted his claim to unlimited rule by virtue of divine right, the whole effort of English libertarians had been to restore the medieval concept of the king being under the law. Hobbes's *Leviathan* struck at the very root of that cause, but it doubtless attracted those who were weary of instability.

The Restoration of the Stuarts in 1660 brought no resolution to the tension between Parliament and king. Opposition to the coronation of a Catholic, James, Duke of York, stimulated the formation of the Whig party with its assertion of Parliamentary authority even over the succession to the throne. It was this party to which Locke's patron, Shaftesbury, attached himself.

The controversy over the succession touched off a new debate over the merits of absolutism. In 1680 there appeared a pamphlet, *Patriarcha*, by Sir Robert Filmer, which renewed the argument that monarchy was divinely ordained and none ought to resist it. Filmer invoked the Bible, singling out God's grant of dominion to Adam as the prototypical institution of a monarchy.

For many years tradition held that Locke intended his two treatises as justification of the Glorious Revolution which deposed James II. He had, however, begun work upon them long before that event. The first treatise was an explicit answer to Filmer. The second set forth Locke's own ideas about the nature of government. The following selections are all from that second and more famous treatise.

Of Civil Government

1. It having been shown in the foregoing discourse (1) That Adam had not, either by natural right of fatherhood, or by positive donation from God, any such authority over his children, or dominion over the world, as is pretended:

(2) That if he had, his heirs yet had no right to it:

(3) That if his heirs had, there being no law of nature or positive law of God that determines which is the right heir in all cases that may arise, the right of succession, and consequently of bearing rule, could not have been certainly determined:

(4) That if even that had been determined, yet the knowledge of which is the eldest line of Adam's posterity being so long since utterly lost, that in the races of mankind and families of the world there remains not to one above another the least pretence to be the eldest house, and to have the right of inheritance:

All these premises having, as I think, been clearly made out, it is impossible that the rulers now on earth should make any benefit, or derive any the least shadow of authority from that, which is held to be the fountain of all power, "Adam's private dominion and paternal jurisdiction;" so that he that will not give just occasion to think that all government in the world is the prod-

From John Locke, *Works* (London: Thomas Tegg; W. Sharpe & Son; G. Offor; G. &. J. Robinson; J. Evans & Co.; Glasgow: R. Griffin & Co.; Dublin; J. Cummin, 1823).

uct only of force and violence, and that men live together by no other rules but that of beasts, where the strongest carries it, and so lay a foundation for perpetual disorder and mischief, tumult, sedition, and rebellion, (things that the followers of that hypothesis so loudly cry out against) must of necessity find out another rise of government, another original of political power, and another way of designing and knowing the persons that have it, than what sir Robert Filmer hath taught us.

2. To this purpose, I think it may not be amiss to set down what I take to be political power; that the power of a magistrate over a subject may be distinguished from that of a father over his children, a master over his servants, a husband over his wife, and a lord over his slave. All which distinct powers happening sometimes together in the same man, if he be considered under these different relations, it may help us to distinguish these powers one from another, and show the difference betwixt a ruler of a commonwealth, a father of a family, and a captain of a galley.

3. Political power, then, I take to be a right of making laws with penalties of death, and consequently all less penalties, for the regulating and preserving of property, and of employing the force of the community, in the execution of such laws, and in the defence of the commonwealth from foreign injury; and all this only for the public good.

Of the State of Nature

4. To understand political power right, and derive it from its original, we must consider what state all men are naturally in, and that is, a state of perfect freedom to order their actions and dispose of their possessions and persons, as they think fit, within the bounds of the law of nature; without asking leave, or depending upon the will of any other man.

A state also of equality, wherein all the power and jurisdiction is reciprocal, no one having more than another; there being nothing more evident than that creatures of the same species and rank, promiscuously born to all the same advantages of nature, and the use of the same faculties, should also be equal one amongst another without subordination or subjection; unless the Lord and Master of them all should, by any manifest declaration of his will, set one above another, and confer on him, by an evident and clear appointment, an undoubted right to dominion and sovereignty.

. . .

6. But though this be a state of liberty, yet it is not a state of licence: though man in that state have an uncontrollable liberty to dispose of his person or possessions, yet he has not liberty to destroy himself, or so much as any creature in his possession, but where some nobler use than its bare preservation calls for it. The state of nature has a law of nature to govern it, which obliges every one: and reason, which is that law, teaches all mankind, who will but consult it, that being all equal and independent, no one ought to harm another in his life, health, liberty, or possessions: for men being all the workmanship of one omnipotent and infinitely wise Maker; all the servants of one sovereign Master, sent into the world by his order, and about his business; they are his property, whose workmanship they are, made to last during his, not another's pleasure: and being furnished with like faculties, sharing all in one community of nature, there cannot be supposed any such subordination among us that may authorize us to destroy another, as if we were made for one another's uses, as the inferior ranks of creatures are for ours. Every one, as he is bound to preserve himself, and not to quit his station wilfully, so by the like reason, when his own preservation comes not in competition, ought he, as much as he can, to preserve the rest of mankind, and may not, unless it be to do justice to an offender, take away or impair the life, or what tends to the preservation of life, the liberty, health, limb, or goods of another.

7. And that all men may be restrained from invading others' rights, and from doing hurt to one another, and the law of nature be observed, which willeth the peace and preservation of all mankind, the execution of the law of nature is, in that state, put into every man's hands, whereby every one has a right to punish the transgressors of that law to such a degree as may hinder its violation: for the law of nature would, as all other laws that concern men in this world, be in vain, if there were nobody that in the state of nature had a power to execute that law, and thereby preserve the innocent, and restrain offenders. And if any one in the state of nature may punish another for any evil he has done, every one may do so: for in that state of perfect equality, where naturally there is no superiority or jurisdiction of one over another, what any

may do in prosecution of that law every one must needs have a right to do.

8. And thus, in the state of nature, "one man comes by a power over another;" but yet no absolute or arbitrary power to use a criminal, when he has got him in his hands, according to the passionate heats or boundless extravagancy of his own will; but only to retribute to him, so far as calm reason and conscience dictate, what is proportionate to his transgression; which is so much as may serve for reparation and restraint: for these two are the only reasons why one man may lawfully do harm to another, which is that we call punishment. In transgressing the law of nature, the offender declares himself to live by another rule than that of reason and common equity, which is that measure God has set to the actions of men for their mutual security; and so he becomes dangerous to mankind, the tie, which is to secure them from injury and violence, being slighted and broken by him: which being a trespass against the whole species, and the peace and safety of it, provided for by the law of nature; every man upon this score, by the right he hath to preserve mankind in general, may restrain, or, where it is necessary, destroy things noxious to them, and so may bring such evil on any one, who hath transgressed that law, as may make him repent the doing of it, and thereby deter him, and by his example others, from doing the like mischief. And in this case, and upon this ground, "every man hath a right to punish the offender, and be executioner of the law of nature."

9. I doubt not but this will seem a very strange doctrine to some men: but, before they condemn it, I desire them to resolve me by what right any prince or state can put to death or punish an alien for any crime he commits in their country. It is certain their laws, by virtue of any sanction they receive from the promulgated will of the legislative, reach not a stranger: they speak not to him, nor, if they did, is he bound to hearken to them. The legislative authority, by which they are in force over the subjects of that commonwealth, hath no power over him. Those who have the supreme power of making laws in England, France, or Holland, are to an Indian but like the rest of the world, men without authority: and therefore, if by the law of nature every man hath not a power to punish offences against it, as he soberly judges the case to require, I see not how the magistrates of any community can punish an alien of another country; since, in reference to him, they can have

no more power than what every man naturally may have over another.

10. Besides the crime which consists in violating the law, and varying from the right rule of reason, whereby a man so far becomes degenerate, and declares himself to quit the principles of human nature, and to be a noxious creature, there is commonly injury done to some person or other, and some other man receives damage by his transgression: in which case he who hath received any damage, has, besides the right of punishment common to him with other men, a particular right to seek reparation from him that has done it: and any other person, who finds it just, may also join with him that is injured, and assist him in recovering from the offender so much as may make satisfaction for the harm he has suffered.

Of the Beginning of Political Societies

95. Men being, as has been said, by nature all free, equal, and independent, no one can be put out of this estate, and subjected to the political power of another, without his own consent. The only way whereby any one divests himself of his natural liberty, and puts on the bonds of civil society, is by agreeing with other men to join and unite into a community, for their comfortable, safe, and peaceable living one amongst another, in a secure enjoyment of their properties, and a greater security against any that are not of it. This any number of men may do, because it injures not the freedom of the rest; they are left as they were in the liberty of the state of nature. When any number of men have so consented to make one community or government, they are thereby presently incorporated, and make one body politic, wherein the majority have a right to act and conclude the rest.

96. For when any number of men have, by the consent of every individual, made a community, they have thereby made that community one body, with a power to act as one body, which is only by the will and determination of the majority; for that which acts any community being only the consent of the individuals of it, and it being necessary to that which is one body to move one way; it is necessary the body should move that way whither the greater force carries it, which is the consent of the majority: or else it is impossible it should act or continue one body, one com-

munity, which the consent of every individual that united into it agreed that it should; and so every one is bound by that consent to be concluded by the majority. And therefore we see that in assemblies, empowered to act by positive laws, where no number is set by that positive law which empowers them, the act of the majority passes for the act of the whole, and of course determines; as having, by the law of nature and reason, the power of the whole.

97. And thus every man, by consenting with others to make one body politic under one government, puts himself under an obligation to every one of that society to submit to the determination of the majority, and to be concluded by it; or else this original compact, whereby he with others incorporate into one society, would signify nothing, and be no compact, if he be left free, and under no other ties than he was in before in the state of nature. For what appearance would there be of any compact? what new engagement, if he were no farther tied by any decrees of the society than he himself thought fit, and did actually consent to? This would be still as great a liberty as he himself had before his compact, or any one else in the state of nature hath, who may submit himself and consent to any acts of it if he thinks fit.

98. For if the consent of the majority shall not, in reason, be received as the act of the whole, and conclude every individual, nothing but the consent of every individual can make anything to be the act of the whole: but such a consent is next to impossible ever to be had, if we consider the infirmities of health, and avocations of business, which in a number, though much less than that of a commonwealth, will necessarily keep many away from the public assembly. To which if we add the variety of opinions, and contrariety of interests which unavoidably happen in all collections of men, the coming into society upon such terms would be only like Cato's coming into the theatre, only to go out again. Such a constitution as this would make the mighty leviathan of a shorter duration than the feeblest creatures, and not let it outlast the day it was born in: which cannot be supposed, till we can think that rational creatures should desire and constitute societies only to be dissolved: for where the majority cannot conclude the rest, there they cannot act as one body, and consequently will be immediately dissolved again.

99. Whosoever therefore out of a state of nature unite into a community, must be understood to give up all the power necessary

to the ends for which they unite into society, to the majority of the community, unless they expressly agreed in any number greater than the majority. And this is done by barely agreeing to unite into one political society, which is all the compact that is, or needs be, between the individuals that enter into, or make up a common-wealth. And thus that which begins and actually constitutes any political society, is nothing but the consent of any number of free-men capable of a majority, to unite and incorporate into such a society. And this is that, and that only, which did or could give beginning to any lawful government in the world.

100. To this I find two objections made.

First, "That there are no instances to be found in story, of a com-pany of men independent and equal one amongst another, that met together, and in this way began and set up a government."

Secondly, "It is impossible of right, that men should do so, be-cause all men being born under government, they are to sumbit to that, and are not at liberty to begin a new one."

101. To the first there is this to answer, that it is not at all to be wondered, that history gives us but a very little account of men that lived together in the state of nature. The inconveniencies of that condition, and the love and want of society, no sooner brought any number of them together, but they presently united and incorpo-rated, if they designed to continue together. And if we may not suppose men ever to have been in the state of nature, because we hear not much of them in such a state, we may as well suppose the armies of Salmanasser or Xerxes were never children, because we hear little of them till they were men, and embodied in armies. Government is every where antecedent to records, and letters seldom come in amongst a people till a long continuation of civil society has, by other more necessary arts, provided for their safety, ease, and plenty: and then they begin to look after the history of their founders, and search into their original, when they have out-lived the memory of it: for it is with commonwealths as with par-ticular persons, they are commonly ignorant of their own births and infancies: and if they know any thing of their original, they are beholden for it to the accidental records that others have kept of it. And those that we have of the beginning of any politics in the world, excepting that of the Jews, where God himself immediately interposed, and which favours not at all paternal dominion, are

all either plain instances of such a beginning as I have mentioned, or at least have manifest footsteps of it.

.   .   .

122. But submitting to the laws of any country, living quietly, and enjoying privileges and protection under them, makes not a man a member of that society: this is only a local protection and homage due to and from all those, who, not being in a state of war, come within the territories belonging to any government, to all parts whereof the force of its laws extends. But this no more makes a man a member of that society, a perpetual subject of that commonwealth, than it would make a man a subject to another, in whose family he found it convenient to abide for some time; though, whilst he continued in it, he were obliged to comply with the laws, and submit to the government he found there. And thus we see, that foreigners, by living all their lives under another government, and enjoying the privileges and protection of it, though they are bound, even in conscience, to submit to its administration, as far forth as any denison; yet do not thereby come to be subjects or members of that commonwealth. Nothing can make any man so, but his actually entering into it by positive engagement, and express promise and compact. This is that which I think concerning the beginning of political societies, and that consent which makes any one a member of any commonwealth.

Of the Ends of Political Society and Government

123. If man in the state of nature be so free as has been said; if he be absolute lord of his own person and possessions, equal to the greatest, and subject to nobody, why will he part with his freedom, why will he give up this empire, and subject himself to the dominion and control of any other power? To which it is obvious to answer, that though in the state of nature he hath such a right, yet the enjoyment of it is very uncertain, and constantly exposed to the invasion of others; for all being kings as much as he, every man his equal, and the greater part no strict observers of equity and justice, the enjoyment of the property he has in this state is very unsafe, very unsecure. This makes him willing to quit a condition, which however free, is full of fears and continual dangers: and it is not without reason that he seeks out, and is willing to join in

society with others, who are already united, or have a mind to unite, for the mutual preservation of their lives, liberties, and estates, which I call by the general name property.

124. The great and chief end, therefore, of men's uniting into commonwealths, and putting themselves under government, is the preservation of their property. To which in the state of nature there are many things wanting.

First, There wants an established, settled, known law, received and allowed by common consent to be the standard of right and wrong, and the common measure to decide all controversies between them: for though the law of nature be plain and intelligible to all rational creatures; yet men being biassed by their interest, as well as ignorant for want of studying it, are not apt to allow of it as a law binding to them in the application of it to their particular cases.

125. Secondly, In the state of nature there wants a known and indifferent judge, with authority to determine all differences according to the established law: for every one in that state being both judge and executioner of the law of nature, men being partial to themselves, passion and revenge is very apt to carry them too far, and with too much heat, in their own cases; as well as negligence and unconcernedness, to make them too remiss in other men's.

126. Thirdly, In the state of nature there often wants power to back and support the sentence when right, and to give it due execution. They who by any injustice offend, will seldom fail, where they are able, by force to make good their injustice; such resistance many times makes the punishment dangerous, and frequently destructive to those who attempt it.

127. Thus mankind, notwithstanding all the privileges of the state of nature, being but in an ill condition, while they remain in it, are quickly driven into society. Hence it comes to pass, that we seldom find any number of men live any time together in this state. The inconveniencies that they are therein exposed to, by the irregular and uncertain exercise of the power every man has of punishing the transgressions of others, make them take sanctuary under the established laws of government, and therein seek the preservation of their property. It is this makes them so willingly give up every one his single power of punishing, to be exercised by such alone as shall be appointed to it amongst them; and by such rules as the

community, or those authorized by them to that purpose, shall agree on. And in this we have the original right of both the legislative and executive power, as well as of the governments and societies themselves.

128. For in the state of nature, to omit the liberty he has of innocent delights, a man has two powers.

The first is to do whatsoever he thinks fit for the preservation of himself and others within the permission of the law of nature: by which law, common to them all, he and all the rest of mankind are one community, make up one society, distinct from all other creatures. And, were it not for the corruption and viciousness of degenerate men, there would be no need of any other; no necessity that men should separate from this great and natural community, and by positive agreements combine into smaller and divided associations.

The other power a man has in the state of nature, is the power to punish the crimes committed against that law. Both these he gives up when he joins in a private, if I may so call it, or particular politic society, and incorporates into any commonwealth, separate from the rest of mankind.

. . .

221. There is therefore, secondly, another way whereby governments are dissolved, and that is, when the legislative, or the prince, either of them, act contrary to their trust.

First, the legislative acts against the trust reposed in them, when they endeavor to invade the property of the subject, and to make themselves, or any part of the community, masters, or arbitrary disposers of the lives, liberties, or fortunes of the people.

222. The reason why men enter into society is the preservation of their property; and the end why they choose and authorize a legislative is, that there may be laws made, and rules set, as guards and fences to the properties of all the members of the society: to limit the power, and moderate the dominion, of every part and member of the society: for since it can never be supposed to be the will of the society that the legislative should have a power to destroy that which every one designs to secure by entering into society, and for which the people submitted themselves to legislators of their own making; whenever the legislators endeavour to take away and destroy the property of the people, or to reduce them to slavery under arbitrary power, they put themselves into a

state of war with the people, who are thereupon absolved from any farther obedience, and are left to the common refuge, which God hath provided for all men, against force and violence. Whensoever therefore the legislative shall transgress this fundamental rule of society; and either by ambition, fear, folly, or corruption, endeavour to grasp themselves, or put into the hands of any other, an absolute power over the lives, liberties, and estates of the people; by this breach of trust they forfeit the power the people had put into their hands for quite contrary ends, and it devolves to the people, who have a right to resume their original liberty, and, by the establishment of a new legislative, (such as they shall think fit) provide for their own safety and security, which is the end for which they are in society. What I have said here, concerning the legislative in general, holds true also concerning the supreme executor, who having a double trust put in him, both to have a part in the legislative, and the supreme execution of the law, acts against both, when he goes about to set up his own arbitrary will as the law of the society. He acts also contrary to his trust, when he either employs the force, treasure, and offices of the society to corrupt the representatives, and gain them to his purposes; or openly pre-engages the electors, and prescribes to their choice, such, whom he has, by solicitations, threats, promises, or otherwise, won to his designs; and employs them to bring in such, who have promised beforehand what to vote, and what to enact. Thus to regulate candidates and electors, and new-model the ways of election, what is it but to cut up the government by the roots, and poison the very fountain of public security? for the people having reserved to themselves the choice of their representatives, as the fence to their properties, could do it for no other end, but that they might always be freely chosen, and so chosen, freely act, and advise, as the necessity of the commonwealth and the public good should, upon examination and mature debate, be judged to require. This, those who give their votes before they hear the debate, and have weighed the reasons on all sides, are not capable of doing. To prepare such an assembly as this, and endeavour to set up the declared abettors of his own will, for the true representatives of the people, and the law-makers of the society, is certainly as great a breach of trust, and as perfect a declaration of a design to subvert the government, as is possible to be met with. To which if one shall add rewards and punishments visibly employed to the same end, and all the arts of perverted law made use of, to take off and destroy all that stand in the way of such a design, and will not comply and consent to betray the liberties of their country, it will be past doubt what is doing. What power they ought to have in the society, who thus employ it contrary to the trust that went along with it in its first institution, is easy to determine; and one cannot but see, that he, who has once attempted any such thing as this, cannot any longer be trusted.

223. To this perhaps it will be said, that the people being ignorant, and always discontented, to lay the foundation of government in the unsteady opinion and uncertain humour of the people, is to expose it to certain ruin; and no government will be able long to subsist, if the people may set up a new legislative, whenever they take offence at the old one. To this I answer, quite the contrary. People are not so easily got out of their old forms, as some are apt to suggest. They are hardly to be prevailed with to amend the acknowledged faults in the frame they have been accustomed to. And if there be any original defects, or adventitious ones introduced by time, or corruption; it is not an easy thing to get them changed, even when all the world sees there is an opportunity for it. This slowness and aversion in the people to quit their old constitutions, has in the many revolutions, which have been seen in this kingdom, in this and former ages, still kept us to, or, after some interval of fruitless attempts, still brought us back again to, our old legislative of king, lords, and commons: and whatever provocations have made the crown be taken from some of our princes' heads, they never carried the people so far as to place it in another line.

224. But it will be said, this hypothesis lays a ferment for frequent rebellion. To which I answer,

First, No more than any other hypothesis: for when the people are made miserable, and find themselves exposed to the ill usage of arbitrary power, cry up their governors as much as you will, for sons of Jupiter; let them be sacred and divine, descended, or authorized from heaven; give them out for whom or what you please, the same will happen. The people generally ill-treated, and contrary to right, will be ready upon any occasion to ease themselves of a burden that sits heavy upon them. They will wish, and seek for the opportunity, which in the change, weakness, and accidents of human affairs, seldom delays long to offer itself. He must have lived but a little while in the world, who has not seen examples of this in his time; and he must have read very little, who cannot produce examples of it in all sorts of governments in the world.

225. Secondly, I answer, such revolutions happen not upon every little mismanagement in public affairs. Great mistakes in the ruling part, many wrong and inconvenient laws, and all the slips of human frailty will be born by the people without mutiny or murmur. But if a long train of abuses, prevarications, and artifices, all tending the same way, make the design visible to the people, and they cannot but feel what they lie under, and see whither they are going; it is not to be wondered, that they should then rouse themselves, and endeavour to put the rule into such hands which may secure to them the ends for which government was at first erected; and without which, ancient names, and specious forms, are so far from being better, that they are much worse, than the state of nature, or pure anarchy; the inconveniencies, being all as great and as near, but the remedy farther off and more difficult.

226. Thirdly, I answer, that this doctrine of a power in the people of providing for their safety anew, by a new legislative, when their legislators have acted contrary to their trust, by invading their property, is the best fence against rebellion, and the probablest means to hinder it: for rebellion being an opposition, not to persons, but authority, which is founded only in the constitutions and laws of the government; those, whoever they be, who by force break through, and by force justify their violation of them, are truly and properly rebels: for when men, by entering into society and civil government, have excluded force, and introduced laws for the preservation of property, peace, and unity amongst themselves; those who set up force again in opposition to the laws, do *rebellare*, that is, bring back again the state of war, and are properly rebels: which they who are in power, (by the pretence they have to authority, the temptation of force they have in their hands, and the flattery of those about them) being likeliest to do; the properest way to prevent the evil is to show them the danger and injustice of it, who are under the greatest temptation to run into it.

. . .

240. Here, it is like, the common question will be made, "Who shall be judge, whether the prince or legislative act contrary to their trust?" This, perhaps, ill-affected and factious men may spread amongst the people, when the prince only makes use of his due prerogative. To this I reply, "The people shall be judge;" for who shall be judge whether his trustee or deputy acts well, and

according to the trust reposed in him, but he who deputes him, and must, by having deputed him, have still a power to discard him, when he fails in his trust? If this be reasonable in particular cases of private men, why should it be otherwise in that of the greatest moment, where the welfare of millions is concerned, and also where the evil, if not prevented, is greater, and the redress very difficult, dear, and dangerous?

241. But farther, this question, ("Who shall be judge?") cannot mean, that there is no judge at all: for where there is no judicature on earth, to decide controversies amongst men, God in heaven is judge. He alone, it is true, is judge of the right. But every man is judge for himself, as in all other cases, so in this, whether another hath put himself into a state of war with him, and whether he should appeal to the supreme Judge, as Jephthah did.

242. If a controversy arise betwixt a prince and some of the people, in a matter where the law is silent or doubtful, and the thing be of great consequence, I should think the proper umpire, in such a case, should be the body of the people: for in cases where the prince hath a trust reposed in him, and is dispensed from the common ordinary rules of the law; there, if any men find themselves aggrieved, and think the prince acts contrary to, or beyond that trust, who so proper to judge as the body of the people, (who, at first, lodged that trust in him) how far they meant it should extend? But if the prince, or whoever they be in the administration, decline that way of determination, the appeal then lies nowhere but to Heaven; force between either persons, who have no known superior on earth, or which permits no appeal to a judge on earth, being properly a state of war, wherein the appeal lies only to Heaven; and in that state the injured party must judge for himself, when he will think fit to make use of that appeal, and put himself upon it.

243. To conclude, The power that every individual gave the society, when he entered into it, can never revert to the individuals again, as long as the society lasts, but will always remain in the community; because without this there can be no community, no commonwealth, which is contrary to the original agreement: so also when the society hath placed the legislative in any assembly of men, to continue in them and their successors, with direction and authority for providing such successors, the legislative can never revert to the people whilst that government lasts; because, having provided a legislative with power to continue for ever, they have

given up their political power to the legislative, and cannot resume it. But if they have set limits to the duration of their legislative, and made this supreme power in any person, or assembly, only temporary; or else, when by the miscarriages of those in authority it is forfeited; upon the forfeiture, or at the determination of the time set, it reverts to the society, and the people have a right to act as supreme, and continue the legislative in themselves; or erect a new form, or under the old form place it in new hands, as they think good.

Samuel Adams: A State of the Rights of the Colonists (1772)

There is no better evidence of Locke's influence upon Americans than the Declaration of Independence. The opening statement of political philosophy is so clearly drawn from Locke that it requires no proof beyond the mere similarities of phraseology. Even before 1776, however, Locke's doctrines of a government founded by compact to protect the rights of the governed suffused American political theory. The polemical literature of the Revolutionary period rested most of its arguments upon Lockean assumptions.

The following selection is from a pamphlet printed by the Boston town meeting in 1772 to arouse the colonists to the dangers inherent in the ministry's attempts to make crown officials independent of colonial control. Its probable author was Samuel Adams (1722–1803).

Natural Rights of the Colonists as Men

Among the natural Rights of the Colonists are these: First, a Right to *Life;* Secondly to *Liberty;* thirdly to *Property;* together with the Right to support and defend them in the best manner they can. Those are evident Branches of, rather than deductions from the Duty of Self Preservation, commonly called the first Law of Nature.

All Men have a Right to remain in a State of Nature as long as they please; And in case of intollerable Oppression, Civil or Religious, to leave the Society they belong to, and enter into another.

When Men enter into Society, it is by voluntary consent; and they have a right to demand and insist upon the performance of such conditions, And previous limitations as form an equitable *original compact.*

From *The Writings of Samuel Adams*, ed. Harry Alonzo Cushing (New York: G. P. Putnam's Sons, 1906), vol. II, pp. 351–55.

Every natural Right not expressly given up or from the nature of a Social Compact necessarily ceded remains.

All positive and civil laws, should conform as far as possible, to the Law of natural reason and equity.

As neither reason requires, nor religion permits the contrary, every Man living in or out of a state of civil society, has a right peaceably and quietly to worship God according to the dictates of his conscience.

"Just and true liberty, equal and impartial liberty" in matters spiritual and temporal, is a thing that all Men are clearly entitled to, by the eternal and immutable laws Of God and nature, as well as by the law of Nations, & all well grounded municipal laws, which must have their foundation in the former.

In regard to Religeon, mutual tolleration in the different professions thereof, is what all good and candid minds in all ages have ever practiced; and both by precept and example inculcated on mankind. And it is now generally agreed among christians that this spirit of toleration in the fullest extent consistent with the being of civil society "is the chief characteristical mark of the true church" & In so much that Mr. Lock has asserted, and proved beyond the possibility of contradiction on any solid ground, that such tolleration ought to be extended to all whose doctrines are not subversive of society. The only Sects which he thinks ought to be, and which by all wise laws are excluded from such toleration, are those who teach Doctrines subversive of the Civil Government under which they live. The Roman Catholicks or Papists are excluded by reason of such Doctrines as these "that Princes excommunicated may be deposed, and those they call *Hereticks* may be destroyed without mercy; besides their recognizing the Pope in so absolute a manner, in subversion of Government, by introducing as far as possible into the states, under whose protection they enjoy life, liberty and property, that solecism in politicks, Imperium in imperio leading directly to the worst anarchy and confusion, civil discord, war and blood shed.

The natural liberty of Men by entring into society is abridg'd or restrained so far only as is necessary for the Great end of Society the best good of the whole.

In the state of nature, every man is under God, Judge and sole Judge, of his own rights and the injuries done him. By entering into society, he agrees to an Arbiter or indifferent Judge between him and his neighbours; but he no more renounces his original right, than by taking a cause out of the ordinary course of law, and leaving the decision to Referees or indifferent Arbitrations. In the last case he must pay the Referees for time and trouble; he should be also willing to pay his Just quota for the support of government, the law and constitution; the end of which is to furnish indifferent and impartial Judges in all cases that may happen, whether civil, ecclesiastical, marine or military.

"The natural liberty of man is to be free from any superior power on earth, and not to be under the will or legislative authority of man; but only to have the law of nature for his rule."

In the state of nature men may as the *Patriarchs* did, employ hired servants for the defence of their lives, liberty and property; and they should pay them reasonable wages. Government was instituted for the purposes of common defence; and those who hold the reins of government have an equitable natural right to an honourable support from the same principle "that the labourer is worthy of his hire" but then the same community which they serve, ought to be assessors of their pay: Governors have no right to seek what they please; by this, instead of being content with the station assigned them, that of honourable servants of the society, they would soon become Absolute masters, Despots, and Tyrants. Hence as a private man has a right to say, what wages he will give in his private affairs, so has a Community to determine what they will give and grant of their Substance, for the Administration of publick affairs. And in both cases more are ready generally to offer their Service at the proposed and stipulated price, than are able and willing to perform their duty.

In short it is the greatest absurdity to suppose it in the power of one or any number of men at the entering into society, to renounce their essential natural rights, or the means of preserving those rights when the great end of civil government from the very nature of its institution is for the support, protection and defence of those very rights: the principal of which as is before observed, are life, liberty and property. If men through fear, fraud or mistake, should *in terms* renounce & give up any essential natural right, the eternal law of reason and the great end of society, would absolutely vacate such renunciation; the right to freedom being *the gift* of God Almighty, it is not in the power of Man to alienate this gift, and voluntarily become a slave.

Chapter IV

Eighteenth-Century Deism

The work of Newton and Locke affected religious as well as political and scientific thought. Newton's mechanical universe had no need of an omnipresent God to keep it in operation; indeed, divine interference contrary to natural law appeared irrational and therefore incredible. Locke's "Essay Concerning Human Understanding" reshaped man's view of human nature and raised doubts about such doctrines as original sin. Yet neither Locke nor Newton set out to attack religious orthodoxy. Indeed, in 1695 Locke published *The Reasonableness of Christianity* to show that the traditional beliefs were credible because they comported with reason. This argument contained within it, however, the seeds of a more radical approach. If reason was the test of faith, then men were at liberty to throw out all that seemed to them irrational—and such was the desire of the deists.

The early English deists were relatively obscure men, but one of their leaders was Matthew Tindal (1657–1733). A lawyer rather than a theologian, Tindal held a doctorate in civil law from Oxford and became a consultant on international law. His family and education at first predisposed him to High Church sentiments, so much so that in 1685, on the succession of James II, he became a Catholic. The coincidence of his conversion with the award of his doctorate, his admission to Doctor's Commons, and the accession of a new and avowedly Catholic monarch suggests political opportunism. Tindal himself was later to attribute it to naïveté.

In 1688 he returned to the Anglican fold and thereafter began to move to the other extreme in doctrinal matters. In 1706 he published an attack upon the pretensions of the priesthood which so angered Commons that it ordered the hangman publicly to burn the book. In the next several years he became ever more closely associated with the religious radicals until, in 1730, he published his most famous work, *Christianity as Old as the Creation*. In ensuing years this work attracted so much attention that it received no less than thirty answers from the defenders of orthodoxy.

Matthew Tindal: Christianity as Old as the Creation (1730)

I desire no more than to be allow'd, That there's a Religion of Nature and Reason written in the Hearts of every One of us from the first Creation; by which all Mankind must judge of the Truth of any instituted Religion whatever; and if it varies from the Religion of Nature and Reason in any one Particular, nay, in the minutest Circumstance, That alone is an Argument, which makes all Things else that can be said for its Support totally ineffectual. If so, must not Natural Religion and external Revelation, like two Tallies, exactly answer one another; without any other Difference between them, but as to the Manner of their being deliver'd? And how can it be otherwise? Can Laws be imperfect, where a Legislator is absolutely perfect? Can Time discover any Thing to him, which he did not foresee from Eternity? And as his Wisdom is always the same, so is his Goodness; and consequently from the Consideration of both these his Laws must always be the same.— Is it not from the infinite Wisdom and Goodness of God, that you suppose the Gospel a most perfect Law, incapable of being repeal'd, or alter'd, or of having Additions; and must not you own the Law of Nature as perfect a Law, except you will say, that God did not arrive to the Perfection of Wisdom and Goodness till about seventeen Hundred Years since.

To plead, That the Gospel is incapable of any Additions, be-

From Matthew Tindal, *Christianity as Old as the Creation* (London, 1730), pp. 60–61, 14–19.

cause the Will of God is immutable, and his Law too perfect to need them, is an Argument, was Christianity a new Religion, which destroys itself, since from the Time it commenc'd, you must own God is mutable; and that such Additions have been made to the All-perfect Laws of infinite Wisdom, as constitute a New Religion. The Reason why the Law of Nature is immutable, is, because it is founded on the unalterable Reason of Things; but if God is an arbitrary Being, and can command Things meerly from Will and Pleasure; some Things toDay, and other toMorrow; there is nothing either in the Nature of God, or in the Things themselves, to hinder him from perpetually changing his Mind. If he once commanded Things without Reason, there can be no Reason why he may not endlessly change such Commands.

. . .

I suppose you will allow, That 'tis evident by the Light of Nature that there is a God; or in other Words, a Being absolutely perfect, and infinitely happy in himself, who is the Source of all other Beings; and that what Perfections soever the Creatures have, they are wholly deriv'd from him.

. . .

Since then, it is demonstrable there is such a Being, it is equally demonstrable, that the Creatures can neither add to, or take from the Happiness of That Being; and that he cou'd have no Motive in Framing his Creatures, or in giving Laws to such of them as he made capable of knowing his Will, but their own Good.

To imagine he created them at first for his own sake, and has since requir'd Things of them for that Reason, is to suppose he was not perfectly happy in himself before the Creation; and that the Creatures, by either observing, or not observing the Rules prescrib'd them, cou'd add to, or take from his Happiness.

If then, a Being infinitely happy in himself, cou'd not command his Creatures any Thing for his own Good; nor an All-wise Being Things to no End or Purpose; nor an All-good Being any Thing but for their Good; it unavoidably follows, nothing can be a Part of the Divine Law, but what tends to promote the common Interest, and mutual Happiness of his rational Creatures; and every Thing that does so must be a Part of it.

As God can require nothing of us, but what makes for our Happiness; so he, who can't envy us any Happiness our Nature is capable of, can forbid us those Things only, which tend to our Hurt; and this we are as certain of, as that there is a God infinitely happy in himself, infinitely good and wise; and as God can design nothing by his Laws but our Good, so by being infinitely powerful, he can bring every Thing to pass which he designs for that End.

From the Consideration of these Perfections, we cannot but have the highest Veneration, nay, the greatest Adoration and Love for this supreme Being; who, that we may not fail to be as happy as possible for such Creatures to be, has made our acting for our *present*, to be the only Means of obtaining our *future* Happiness; and that we can't sin against him, but by acting against our reasonable Natures: These Reflections, which occur to every One who in the least considers, must give us a wonderful and surprizing Sense of the divine Goodness, fill us with Admiration, Transport and Extacy (of which we daily see among contemplative Persons remarkable Instances) and not only force us to express a never-failing Gratitude in Raptures of the highest Praise and Thanksgiving; but make us strive to imitate him in our extensive Love to our Fellow-Creatures: And Thus copying after the Divine Original, and taking God himself for our Precedent, must make us like unto him, who is all Perfection and all Happiness; and who must have an inexhaustible Love for all, who thus endeavour to imitate him.

The Difference between the Supreme Being, infinitely happy in himself, and the Creatures who are not so, is, That all his Actions, in Relation to his Creatures, flow from a pure disinterested Love; whereas the Spring of all the Actions of the Creatures is their own Good.: *We love God, because he first lov'd us;* and consequently, our Love to him will be in Proportion to our Sense of his Goodness to us. And therefore, we can't in the least vary from those Sentiments, which the Consideration of the divine Attributes implant in us; but we must in Proportion take off from the Goodness of God, and those Motives we have to love him as we ought.

Our Reason, which gives us a Demonstration of the Divine Perfections, affords us the same concerning the Nature of those Duties God requires; not only with Relation to himself, but to ourselves, and one another: Those we shall discern, if we look into ourselves, and consider our own Natures, and those Circumstances God has plac'd us in with Relation to our Fellow-Creatures; and see what conduces to our mutual Happiness: Of This, our Senses, our Reason, the Experience of Others as well as our own, can't fail to give us sufficient Information.

With relation to ourselves, we can't but know how we are to act;

if we consider, that God has endow'd Man with such a Nature, as makes him necessarily desire his own Good; and, therefore, he may be sure, that God, who has bestow'd this Nature on him, cou'd not require any Thing of him in Prejudice of it; but on the contrary, that he shou'd do every Thing which tends to promote the Good of it. The Health of the Body, and the Vigor of the Mind being highly conducing to our Good, we must be sensible we offend our Maker, if we indulge our Senses to the Prejudice of These: And because not only all irregular Passions, all unfriendly Affections carry their own Torment with them, and endless Inconveniences attend the Excess of sensual Delights; and all immoderate Desires (human Nature being able to bear but a certain Proportion) disorder both Mind and Body; we can't but know we ought to use great Moderation with Relation to our Passions, or in other Words, govern all our Actions by Reason; That, and our True Interest being inseparable. And in a Word, whoever so regulates his natural Appetites, as will conduce most to the Exercise of his Reason, the Health of his Body, and the Pleasure of his Senses, taken and consider'd together, (since herein his Happiness consists) may be certain he can never offend his Maker; Who, as he governs all Things according to their Natures, can't but expect his rational Creatures shou'd act according to their Natures.

As to what God expects from Man with relation to each other; every One must know his Duty, who considers that the common Parent of Mankind has the whole Species alike under his Protection, and will equally punish him for injuring others, as he would others for injuring him; and consequently, that it is his Duty to deal with them, as he expects they should deal with him in the like Circumstances. How much this is his Duty every One must perceive, who considers himself as a weak Creature, not able to subsist without the Assistance of others, who have it in their Power to retaliate the Usage he gives them: And that he may expect, if he breaks those Rules which are necessary for Mens mutual Happiness, to be treated like a common Enemy, not only by the Persons injur'd, but by all others; who, by the common Ties of Nature, are oblig'd to defend, and assist each other. And not only a Man's own particular Interest, but that of his Children, his Family, and all that's dear to him, obliges him to promote the common Happiness, and to endeavour to convey the same to Posterity.

All *Moralists* agree, that human Nature is so constituted, that Men can't live without Society and mutual Assistance; and that

God has endow'd them with Reason, Speech, and other Faculties; evidently fitted to enable them to assist each other in all Matters of Life; That, therefore, 'tis the Will of God who gives them this Nature, and endows them with these Faculties, that they should employ them for their common Benefit and mutual Assistance. And the *Philosophers*, who saw that all Society would be dissolv'd, and Men soon become destitute of even the Necessaries of Life, and be a Prey to one another, if each Man was only to mind himself, and his own single Interest; and that every Thing pointed out the Necessity of mutual Benevolence among Mankind; and therefore they judg'd, that Men by their Nature were fram'd to be useful to one another; *Ad tuendos conservandosq; homines hominem natum esse*, says *Cicero*. And therefore, every Man, for the sake of others as well as himself, is not to disable his Body or Mind by such Irregularities, as may make him less serviceable to them.

In short, considering the Variety of Circumstances Men are under, and these continually changing, as well as being for the most Part unforeseen; 'tis impossible to have Rules laid down by any *External* Revelation for every particular Case; and therefore, there must be some standing Rule, discoverable by the *Light of Nature*, to direct us in all such Cases. And we can't be more certain that 'tis the Will of God, that those Effects which flow from Natural Causes shou'd so flow, than we are that 'tis the Will of God, that Men shou'd observe whatever the Nature of Things, and the Relation they have to one another make fit to be observ'd, shou'd be so observ'd; Or in other Words, we can't but know, if we in the least consider, that whatever Circumstances Men are plac'd in, by the universal Cause of all Things; that 'tis his eternal and immutable Will, by his placing them in these Circumstances, that they act as These require. 'Tis absurd to imagine we are oblig'd to act Thus in some Cases, and not in others; when the Reason for acting Thus in all is the same. This Consideration alone will direct a Man how to act in all Conditions of Life, whether *Father, Son, Husband, Servant, Subject, Master, King, &c.* Thus we see how the Reason of Things, or the Relation they have to each other, teaches us our Duty in all Cases whatever. And I may add, that the better to cause Men to observe those Rules, which make for their mutual Benefit, infinite Goodness has sown in their Hearts Seeds of Pity, Humanity and Tenderness, which, without much Difficulty, cannot be eradicated; but nothing operates more strongly than that Desire Men have of being in Esteem, Credit, and Reputation with their

Fellow Creatures; not to be obtain'd without acting on the Principles of Natural Justice, Equity, Benevolence, &c.

In a Word, As a most beneficent Disposition in the Supreme Being is the Source of all his Actions in relation to his Creatures; so he has implanted in Man, whom he has made after his own Image, a Love for his Species; the gratifying of which in doing Acts of Benevolence, Compassion and good Will, produces a Pleasure that never satiates; as on the contrary, Actions of Ill Nature, Envy, Malice, &c. never fail to produce Shame, Confusion, and everlasting Self-Reproach.

Voltaire: Philosophical Dictionary (1764)

Deism began as an English movement, but it soon crossed the channel to Europe, where its foremost proponent was François Marie Arouet, more commonly known as Voltaire (1694–1778). A prominent French literary figure, Voltaire was regularly in difficulties because of his lampoons of political leaders. In 1726 his involvement in an illegal duel led to exile in England, where he imbibed the English Enlightenment. Already of liberal views, he returned to his homeland to divide his time between amatory adventures, literary activities, and popularizing the views of Locke, Newton, and the deists. Although he may already have developed deistical tendencies on his own, his sojourn in England no doubt strengthened them, while the English toleration for dissent aroused his admiration. From a sanctuary near the Swiss border he spread his views through novels, poetry, plays, and a voluminous correspondence with such luminaries as Frederick the Great of Prussia.

In 1764 he published his *Philosophical Dictionary*. In all his works, wit, irony, and sarcasm were his most effective tools, and in the *Dictionary* he repeatedly turned them against his favorite target, institutionalized religion.

God—Gods

The reader cannot too carefully bear in mind that this dictionary has not been written for the purpose of repeating what so many others have said.

From Voltaire, *Works* (New York: Hubert Gould, 1901), vol. V, pp. 212–16, 248–52; vol. VII, pp. 61–63.

The knowledge of a God is not impressed upon us by the hands of nature, for then men would all have the same idea: and no idea is born with us. It does not come to us like the perception of light, of the ground, etc., which we receive as soon as our eyes and our understandings are opened. Is it a philosophical idea? No; men admitted the existence of gods before they were philosophers.

Whence, then, is this idea derived? From feeling, and from that natural logic which unfolds itself with age, even in the rudest of mankind. Astonishing effects of nature were beheld—harvests and barrenness, fair weather and storms, benefits and scourges; and the hand of a master was felt. Chiefs were necessary to govern societies; and it was needful to admit sovereigns of these new sovereigns whom human weakness had given itself—beings before whose power these men who could bear down their fellow-men might tremble. The first sovereigns in their time employed these notions to cement their power. Such were the first steps; thus every little society had its god. These notions were rude because everything was rude. It is very natural to reason by analogy. One society under a chief did not deny that the neighboring tribe should likewise have its judge, or its captain; consequently it could not deny that the other should also have its god. But as it was to the interest of each tribe that its captain should be the best, it was also interested in believing, and consequently it did believe, that its god was the mightiest. Hence those ancient fables which have so long been generally diffused, that the gods of one nation fought against the gods of another. Hence the numerous passages in the Hebrew books, which we find constantly disclosing the opinion entertained by the Jews, that the gods of their enemies existed, but that they were inferior to the God of the Jews.

Meanwhile, in the great states where the progress of society allowed to individuals the enjoyment of speculative leisure, there were priests, Magi, and philosophers.

Some of these perfected their reason so far as to acknowledge in secret one only and universal god. So, although the ancient Egyptians adored Osiri, Osiris, or rather Osireth (which signifies this land is mine); though they also adored other superior beings, yet they admitted one supreme, one only principal god, whom they called "*Knef*," whose symbol was a sphere placed on the frontispiece of the temple.

After this model, the Greeks had their Zeus, their Jupiter, the master of the other gods, who were but what the angels are with the Babylonians and the Hebrews, and the saints with the Christians of the Roman communion.

It is a more thorny question than it has been considered, and one by no means profoundly examined, whether several gods, equal in power, can exist at the same time?

We have no adequate idea of the Divinity; we creep on from conjecture to conjecture, from likelihood to probability. We have very few certainties. There is something; therefore there is something eternal; for nothing is produced from nothing. Here is a certain truth on which the mind reposes. Every work which shows us means and an end, announces a workman; then this universe, composed of springs, of means, each of which has its end, discovers a most mighty, a most intelligent workman. Here is a probability approaching the greatest certainty. But is this supreme artificer infinite? Is he everywhere? Is he in one place? How are we, with our feeble intelligence and limited knowledge, to answer these questions?

My reason alone proves to me a being who has arranged the matter of this world; but my reason is unable to prove to me that he made this matter—that he brought it out of nothing. All the sages of antiquity, without exception, believed matter to be eternal, and existing by itself. All then that I can do, without the aid of superior light, is to believe that the God of this world is also eternal, and existing by Himself. God and matter exist by the nature of things. May not other gods exist, as well as other worlds? Whole nations, and very enlightened schools, have clearly admitted two gods in this world—one the source of good, the other the source of evil. They admitted an eternal war between two equal powers. Assuredly, nature can more easily suffer the existence of several independent beings in the immensity of space, than that of limited and powerless gods in this world of whom one can do no good, and the other no harm.

If God and matter exist from all eternity, as antiquity believed, here then are two necessary beings; now, if there be two necessary beings, there may be thirty. These doubts alone, which are the germ of an infinity of reflections, serve at least to convince us of the feebleness of our understanding. We must, with Cicero, confess our ignorance of the nature of the Divinity; we shall never know any more of it than he did.

In vain do the schools tell us that God is infinite negatively and not privatively—"*formaliter et non materialiter*," that He is the first act, the middle, and the last—that He is everywhere without being in any place; a hundred pages of commentaries on definitions like these cannot give us the smallest light. We have no steps whereby to arrive at such knowledge.

We feel that we are under the hand of an invisible being; this is all; we cannot advance one step farther. It is mad temerity to seek to divine what this being is—whether he is extended or not, whether he is in one place or not, how he exists, or how he operates.

. . .

In the reign of Arcadius, Logomachos, a theologue of Constantinople, went into Scythia and stopped at the foot of Mount Caucasus in the fruitful plains of Zephirim, on the borders of Colchis. The good old man Dondindac was in his great hall between his large sheepfold and his extensive barn; he was on his knees with his wife, his five sons and five daughters, his kinsmen and servants; and all were singing the praises of God, after a light repast. "What are you doing, idolater?" said Logomachos to him. "I am not an idolater," said Dondindac. "You must be an idolater," said Logomachos, "for you are not a Greek. Come, tell me what you were singing in your barbarous Scythian jargon?" "All tongues are alike to the ears of God," answered the Scythian; "we were singing His praises." "Very extraordinary!" returned the theologue; "a Scythian family praying to God without having been instructed by us!" He soon entered into conversation with the Scythian Dondindac; for the theologue knew a little Scythian, and the other a little Greek. This conversation has been found in a manuscript preserved in the library of Constantinople.

LOGOMACHOS.

Let us see if you know your catechism. Why do you pray to God?

DONDINDAC.

Because it is just to adore the Supreme Being, from whom we have everything.

LOGOMACHOS.

Very fair for a barbarian. And what do you ask of him?

DONDINDAC.

I thank Him for the blessings I enjoy, and even for the trials which He sends me; but I am careful to ask nothing of Him; for

He knows our wants better than we do; besides, I should be afraid of asking for fair weather while my neighbor was asking for rain.

LOGOMACHOS.

Ah! I thought he would say some nonsense or other. Let us begin farther back. Barbarian, who told you that there is a God?

DONDINDAC.

All nature tells me.

LOGOMACHOS.

That is not enough. What idea have you of God?

DONDINDAC.

The idea of my Creator; my master, who will reward me if I do good, and punish me if I do evil.

LOGOMACHOS.

Trifles! trash! Let us come to some essentials. Is God *infinite secundum quid*, or according to essence?

DONDINDAC.

I don't understand you.

LOGOMACHOS.

Brute beast! Is God in one place, or in every place?

DONDINDAC.

I know not . . . . just as you please.

LOGOMACHOS.

Ignoramus! . . . . Can He cause that which has not been to have been, or that a stick shall not have two ends? Does He see the future as future, or as present? How does He draw being from nothing, and how reduce being to nothing?

DONDINDAC.

I have never examined these things.

LOGOMACHOS.

What a stupid fellow! Well, I must come nearer to your level. . . . Tell me, friend, do you think that matter can be eternal?

DONDINDAC.

What matters it to me whether it exists from all eternity or not? I do not exist from all eternity. God must still be my Master. He has given me the nature of justice; it is my duty to follow it: I seek not to be a philosopher; I wish to be a man.

LOGOMACHOS.

One has a great deal of trouble with these blockheads. Let us proceed step by step. What is God?

DONDINDAC.

My sovereign, my judge, my father.

LOGOMACHOS.

That is not what I ask. What is His nature?

DONDINDAC.

To be mighty and good.

LOGOMACHOS.

But is He corporeal or spiritual?

DONDINDAC.

How should I know that?

LOGOMACHOS.

What; do you not know what a spirit is?

DONDINDAC.

Not in the least. Of what service would that knowledge be to me? Should I be more just? Should I be a better husband, a better father, a better master, or a better citizen?

LOGOMACHOS.

You must absolutely be taught what a spirit is. It is—it is—it is—I will say what another time.

DONDINDAC.

I much fear that you will tell me rather what it is not than what it is. Permit me, in turn, to ask you one question. Some time ago, I saw one of your temples: why do you paint God with a long beard?

LOGOMACHOS.

That is a very difficult question, and requires preliminary instruction.

DONDINDAC.

Before I receive your instruction, I must relate to you a thing which one day happened to me. I had just built a closet at the end of my garden, when I heard a mole arguing thus with an ant: "Here is a fine fabric," said the mole; "it must have been a very powerful mole that performed this work." "You jest," returned the ant; "the architect of this edifice is an ant of mighty genius." From that time I resolved never to dispute.

Religion

The Epicureans, who had no religion, recommended retirement from public affairs, study, and concord. This sect was a society of friends, for friendship was their principal dogma. Atticus, Lucretius, Memmius, and a few other such men, might live very reputably together; this we see in all countries; philosophize as much as you please among yourselves. A set of amateurs may give a concert of refined and scientific music; but let them beware of performing such a concert before the ignorant and brutal vulgar, lest their instruments be broken over their heads. If you have but a village to govern, it *must* have a religion.

I speak not here of an error; but of the only good, the only necessary, the only proved, and the second revealed.

Had it been possible for the human mind to have admitted a religion—I will not say at all approaching ours—but not so bad as all the other religions in the world—what would that religion have been?

Would it not have been that which should propose to us the adoration of the supreme, only, infinite, eternal Being, the former of the world, who gives it motion and life, *"cui nec simile, nec secundum"*? That which should re-unite us to this Being of beings, as the reward of our virtues, and separate us from Him, as the chastisement of our crimes?

That which should admit very few of the dogmas invented by unreasoning pride; those eternal subjects of disputation; and should teach a pure morality, about which there should never be any dispute?

That which should not make the essence of worship consist in vain ceremonies, as that of spitting into your mouth, or that of taking from you one end of your prepuce, or of depriving you of one of your testicles—seeing that a man may fulfil all the social duties with two testicles and an entire foreskin, and without another's spitting into his mouth?

That of serving one's neighbor for the love of God, instead of persecuting and butchering him in God's name? That which should tolerate all others, and which, meriting thus the goodwill of all, should alone be capable of making mankind a nation of brethren?

That which should have august ceremonies, to strike the vulgar, without having mysteries to disgust the wise and irritate the incredulous?

That which should offer men more encouragements to the social virtues than expiations for social crimes?

That which should insure to its ministers a revenue large enough for their decent maintenance, but should never allow them to usurp dignities and power that might make them tyrants?

That which should establish commodious retreats for sickness and old age, but never for idleness?

Benjamin Franklin: ". . . My Religion" (1790)

Deistical works such as those of Tindal and Voltaire appeared on lists of many colonial libraries in the eighteenth century. Many members of the upper class adhered to deistic beliefs, among them the most famous American proponent of the Enlightenment, Benjamin Franklin. The following selection is from a letter Franklin wrote near the end of his life to Ezra Stiles, president of Yale, who had asked Franklin about his religious convictions. In his reply Franklin summed up what was the creed of most deists, European and American.

You desire to know something of my Religion. It is the first time I have been questioned upon it. But I cannot take your Curiosity amiss, and shall endeavour in a few Words to gratify it. Here is my Creed. I believe in one God, Creator of the Universe. That he governs it by his Providence. That he ought to be worshipped. That the most acceptable Service we render to him is doing good to his other Children. That the soul of Man is immortal, and will be treated with Justice in another Life respecting its Conduct in this. These I take to be the fundamental Principles of all sound Religion, and I regard them as you do in whatever Sect I meet with them.

As to Jesus of Nazareth, my Opinion of whom you particularly

From Benjamin Franklin to Ezra Stiles, March 9, 1790, in *The Works of Benjamin Franklin*, ed. John Bigelow (New York: G. P. Putnam's Sons, 1904), vol. XII, pp. 185–86.

desire, I think the System of Morals and his Religion, as he left them to us, the best the World ever saw or is likely to see; but I apprehend it has received various corrupting Changes, and I have, with most of the present Dissenters in England, some Doubts as to his Divinity; tho' it is a question I do not dogmatize upon, having never studied it, and think it needless to busy myself with it now, when I expect soon an Opportunity of knowing the Truth with less Trouble. I see no harm, however, in its being believed, if that Belief has the good Consequence, as probably it has, of making his Doctrines more respected and better observed; especially as I do not perceive, that the Supreme takes it amiss, by distinguishing the Unbelievers in his Government of the World with any peculiar Marks of his Displeasure.

I shall only add, respecting myself, that, having experienced the Goodness of that Being in conducting me prosperously thro' a long life, I have no doubt of its Continuance in the next, though without the smallest Conceit of meriting such Goodness.

Thomas Jefferson: The Life and Morals of Jesus Christ (c. 1817–19)

Another prominent American deist was Thomas Jefferson, who composed his own version of the New Testament by cutting up the four gospels and pasting together the verses to form a connected narrative of the life of Jesus. The result is as interesting for what is left out as for what is included. The title, *The Life and Morals of Jesus Christ of Nazareth*, reflects the typical emphasis of the eighteenth century on the moral teaching of Christianity. The following selections deal with the nativity and death of Jesus, and the very last sentence of these excerpts is the last sentence in Jefferson's work.

Luke ii:

1   And it came to pass in those days, that there went out a decree from Caesar Augustus, that all the world should be taxed.

2   (*And* this taxing was first made when Cyrenius was governor of Syria.)

3   And all went to be taxed, every one into his own city.

From Thomas Jefferson, *The Life and Morals of Jesus Christ of Nazareth*, with an introduction by Cyrus Adler (Washington: U.S. Government Printing Office, 1904), pp. 1, 81–82.

4   And Joseph also went up from Galilee, out of the city of Nazareth, into Judea unto the city of David, which is called Bethlehem; (because he was of the house and lineage of David:)

5   To be taxed with Mary his espoused wife, being great with child.

6   And so it was, that, while they were there, the days were accomplished that she should be delivered.

7   And she brought forth her first-born son, and wrapped him in swaddling clothes, and laid him in a manger; because there was no room for them in the inn.

21   And when eight days were accomplished for the circumcising of the child, his name was called JESUS,

39   And when they had performed all things according to the law of the Lord, they returned into Galilee, to their own city Nazareth.

. . .

John XIX:

25   Now there stood by the cross of Jesus his mother, and his mother's sister, Mary the *wife* of Cleophas, and Mary Magdalene.

26   When Jesus therefore saw his mother, and the disciple standing by, whom he loved, he saith unto his mother, Woman, behold thy son!

27   Then saith he to the disciple, Behold thy mother! And from that hour that disciple took her unto his own *home*.

Matthew XXVII:

46   And about the ninth hour Jesus cried with a loud voice, saying, Eli, Eli, lama, sabachthani? that is to say, My God, My God, why hast thou forsaken me?

47   Some of them that stood there, when they heard *that*, said, This *man* calleth for Elias.

48   And straightway one of them ran, and took a sponge, and filled *it* with vinegar and put *it* on a reed, and gave him to drink.

49   The rest said, Let be, let us see whether Elias will come to save him.

50   Jesus, when he had cried again with a loud voice, yielded up the ghost.

55   And many women were there beholding afar off, which followed Jesus from Galilee, ministering unto him.

56   Among which was Mary Magdalene, and Mary the mother of James and Joses, and the mother of Zebedee's children.

John xix:

31   The Jews therefore, because it was the preparation, that the bodies should not remain upon the cross on the sabbath day, (for that sabbath day was an high day,) besought Pilate that their legs might be broken, and *that* they might be taken away.

32   Then came the soldiers, and brake the legs of the first and of the other which was crucified with him.

33   But when they came to Jesus, and saw that he was dead already, they brake not his legs:

34   But one of the soldiers with a spear pierced his side, and forthwith came thereout blood and water.

38   And after this Joseph of Arimathæa, being a disciple of Jesus, but secretly for fear of the Jews, besought Pilate that he might take away the body of Jesus: and Pilate gave *him* leave. He came therefore, and took the body of Jesus.

39   And there came also Nicodemus, which at the first came to Jesus by night, and brought a mixture of myrrh and aloes, about an hundred pound *weight.*

40   Then took they the body of Jesus, and wound it in linen clothes with the spices, as the manner of the Jews is to bury.

41   Now in the place where he was crucified there was a garden; and in the garden a new sepulchre, wherein was never man yet laid.

42   There laid they Jesus.

Matthew xxvii:

60   And rolled a great stone to the door of the sepulchre, and departed.

Ethan Allen: Reason, the Only Oracle of Man (1784)

Jefferson apparently intended his version of the New Testament for his personal use. Receiving somewhat wider distribution was Ethan Allen's *Reason, the Only Oracle of Man* (1784). While still a youth, Allen began work on the manuscript with a close friend, Dr. Thomas Young, who provided Allen's principal link with the formal learning of the eighteenth century. Their collaboration was interrupted and not until the end of the Revolutionary War did Allen have the time to devote to his philosophical pursuits. By that time Young had died and Allen proceeded to work from the notes they had previously compiled. Many of the original 1,500 copies burned in a fire at the printer's, but the remainder circulated freely. Eventually the book became known in Vermont as "Ethan Allen's Bible." (See also page 53.)

Prayer Cannot Be Attended with Miraculous Consequences

Before we conclude our discourse upon miracles, it will be requisite that we consider those supposed miraculous alterations of nature, or of divine providence, which by some are thought to have taken place in the world, merely in conformity to the prayer of Man. The arguments, which have been already advanced against miracles, are in substance equally applicable, to such as may be supposed to be effectuated by prayers, remonstrances or supplications of finite beings. That God should countermand his order of nature, which is the same thing as to alter his providence, merely in dictatorial conformity to the prayers or praises of his creatures, or that he should alter it merely from motives from himself are not essentially different. In as much as the consequence of a supposed alteration from either of the causes before mentioned would equally and necessarily imply mutability in wisdom, in the one case, as in the other; for in both cases the arguments terminate against any supposed miraculous alterations of nature or providence, merely from the consideration of the immutable perfection of the divine nature. For a departure from, or alteration of the eternal order, or government of things would be equally derogatory from the absolute perfection of God, whether those alterations are supposed to take place merely in conformity to the prayers or remonstrances of his creatures, or from reasons, which may be supposed to have originated merely from the divine mind itself. There is no thing, which can be mentioned, that would more manifestly argue mutability in God, than that he should alter his order of nature or providence to comply with the prayers of his mutable creatures; or to do that in conformity thereto, which the eternal regulation and government of nature would not have effectuated or accomplished independent of them. For if the eternal

From Ethan Allen, *Reason, the Only Oracle of Man* (Bennington, Vt.: Haswell and Russell, 1784).

laws of nature were absolutely perfect, which must be admitted, a deviation from, or countermanding of them, must unavoidably imply mutability and imperfection, be it from what cause it will.

Sensibly to depend upon God in and through his order of nature, to retain in our minds a grateful sense of his providential goodness to us, to place in him our important hope of immortality, and to act and demean ourselves under all circumstances of life agreeable to reason, or the moral rectitude of things pointed out unto us thereby, is our indispensible duty: it is enjoined by the laws of nature and ought to be taught and cultivated among mankind. But prayer to God is no part of a rational religion, nor did reason ever dictate it, but, was it duly attended to, it would teach us the contrary.

To make known our wants to God by prayer or to communicate any intelligence concerning ourselves or the universe to him, is impossible, since his omniscient mind has a perfect knowledge of all things, and therefore is beholden to none of our correspondence to inform himself of our circumstances, or of what would be wisest and best to do for us in all possible conditions and modes of existence, in our never ending duration of being. These, with the infinitude of things, have been eternally deliberated by the omniscient mind, who can admit of no additional intelligence, whether by prayer or otherwise, which renders it nugatory.

We ought to act up to the dignity of our nature, and demean ourselves, as creatures of our rank and capacity in the order of Being ought to do, and not presume to dictate any thing, less or more, to the governor of the universe; who rules not by our proscriptions, but by eternal and infinite reason. To pray to God, or to make supplication to him, requesting certain favors for ourselves, or for any, or all the species, is inconsistent with the relation which subsists between God and man. Whoever has a just sense of the absolute perfection of God, and of their own imperfection, and natural subjection to his providence, cannot but from thence infer the impropriety of praying or supplicating to God, for this, that, or the other thing; or of remonstrating against his providence; inasmuch, as "*known to God are all our wants;*" and as we know, that we ourselves are inadequate judges of what would be best for us, all things considered. God looks through the immensity of things, and understands the harmony, moral beauty and decorum of the whole, and will by no means change his purposes, or alter the nature of the things themselves for any of our intreaties or threats. To pray, intreat, or make supplication to God, is neither more nor less than dictating to Eternal Reason, and entering into the province and prerogative of the Almighty; if this is not the meaning and import of prayer, it has none at all, that extends to the final events and consequences of things. . . .

Chapter V

Montesquieu (1689-1755)

The political theorists of the seventeenth century, such as Locke and Hobbes, built their ideas about the origins and ends of government by relying solely upon "reason." Their "state of nature" and "social contract" were theoretical constructs, lacking any base in historical evidence. The Newtonian revolution, however, stirred men to attempting duplication of Newton's feat in other realms of knowledge. As Newton sought to explain the natural laws of the physical universe, others set out to explain the natural laws governing man's social life.

The first man to attempt a "scientific" approach to political theory was Charles Louis de Secondat, Baron de La Brède et de Montesquieu (1689–1755). Well situated by his inheritance of both a title and an income from his uncle, Montesquieu first attracted the attention of Frenchmen by his publication of *The Persian Letters* (1721). Its imaginary dialogue between two Persians visiting France was a satire on the state of politics, religion, and society, and it set the tone for the subsequent French *philosophe* movement which represented the French Enlightenment. In 1728 he left France to tour the continent, finishing with an eighteen-month stay in England. When he returned to France he took up the apparently placid life of a country gentleman and began work on the book that was to become his greatest contribution.

That book, *The Spirit of Laws* (1748), marked a new departure in the history of political theory because it abandoned the introspective method of the seventeenth century and attempted instead to present empirical evidence from which to elicit general conclusions. Although much of Montesquieu's information was wrong and his methods of inquiry do not conform to the standards of modern research, nevertheless his work represented the first step toward a more scientific investigation of social life. Its concern with the influence of climate and geography on man's political institutions reflected the predominant environmentalist point of view which had sprung from Lockean psychology.

The passage which follows is one of the most famous sections in *The Spirit of Laws*. Montesquieu's view of the English constitution was a misapprehension, yet the theory which it represented was to have great appeal to Americans.

The Spirit of Laws (1748)

Different Significations Given to the Word Liberty

There is no word that has admitted of more various significations, and has made more different impressions on human minds, than that of *liberty*. Some have taken it for a facility of deposing a person on whom they had conferred a tyrannical authority; others for the power of chusing a person whom they are obliged to obey; others for the right of bearing arms, and of being thereby enabled to use violence; others for the privilege of being governed by a native of their own country, or by their own laws.[1] A certain nation thought for a long time that liberty consisted in the privilege of wearing a long beard.[2] Some have annexed this name to one form of government, in exclusion of others: those who had a republican taste, applied it to this government; those who liked a monarchical state, gave it to monarchies.[3] Thus they all have applied the name of liberty to the government most conformable to their own customs and inclinations: and as in a republic people have not so con-

From Charles Louis de Secondat, Baron de Montesquieu, *The Spirit of Laws*, trans. Thomas Nugent (Edinburgh: Silvester Doig, 1793), pp. 162–75.

stant and so present a view of the instruments of the evils they complain of, and likewise as the laws seem there to speak more, and the executors of the laws less, it is generally attributed to republics, and denied to monarchies. In fine, as in democracies the people seem to do very near whatever they please, liberty has been placed in this sort of government, and the power of the people has been confounded with their liberty.

In What Liberty Consists

It is true, that in democracies the people seem to do what they please; but political liberty does not consist in an unrestrained freedom. In governments, that is, in societies directed by laws, liberty can consist only in the power of doing what we ought to will, and in not being constrained to do what we ought not to will.

We must have continually present to our minds the difference between independence and liberty. Liberty is a right of doing whatever the laws permit; and if a citizen could do what they forbid, he would no longer be possessed of liberty, because all his fellow citizens would have the same power.

The Same Subject Continued

Democratic and aristocratic states are not necessarily free. Political liberty is to be met with only in moderate governments: yet even in these it is not always met with. It is there only when there is no abuse of power: but constant experience shows us, that every man invested with power is apt to abuse it; he pushes on till he comes to something that limits him. Is it not strange, though true, to say, that virtue itself has need of limits?

To prevent the abuse of power, it is necessary that by the very disposition of things power should be a check to power. A government may be so constituted, as no man shall be compelled to do things to which the law does not oblige him, nor forced to abstain from things which the law permits.

Of the End or View of Different Governments

Though all governments have the same general end, which is that of preservation, yet each has another particular view. Increase of dominion was the view of Rome; war, of Sparta; religion, of the Jewish laws; commerce, that of Marseilles; public tranquillity, that of the laws of China;[4] navigation, that of the laws of Rhodes; natural liberty, that of the policy of the savages; in general, the pleasures of the prince that of despotic states; that of monarchies, the prince's and the kingdom's glory: the independence of individuals, is the end aimed at by the laws of Poland, and from thence results the oppression of the whole.[5]

One nation there is also in the world, that has for the direct end of its constitution political liberty. We shall examine presently the principles on which this liberty is founded: if they are found, liberty will appear as in a mirrour.

To discover political liberty in a constitution, no great labour is requisite. If we are capable of seeing it where it exists, why should we go any further in search of it?

Of the Constitution of England

In every government there are three sorts of power: the legislative; the executive, in respect to things dependent on the law of nations; and the executive, in regard to things that depend on the civil law.

By virtue of the first, the prince or magistrate enacts temporary or perpetual laws, and amends or abrogates those that have been already enacted. By the second, he makes peace or war, sends or receives embassies, establishes the public security, and provides against invasions. By the third, he punishes criminals, or determines the disputes that arise between individuals. The latter we shall call the judiciary power, and the other simply the executive power of the state.

The political liberty of the subject is a tranquility of mind, arising from the opinion each person has of his safety. In order to have this liberty, it is requisite the government be so constituted as one man need not be afraid of another.

When the legislative and executive powers are united, in the person, or in the same body of magistrates, there can be no liberty; because apprehensions may arise, lest the same monarch or senate should enact tyrannical laws, to execute them in a tyrannical manner.

Again, there is no liberty, if the power of judging be not separated from the legislative and executive powers. Were it joined with the legislative, the life and liberty of the subject would be exposed to arbitrary controul; for the judge would then be the legislator. Were it joined to the executive power, the judge might behave with all the violence of an oppressour.

There would be an end of every thing, were the same man, or the same body, whether of the nobles or of the people to exercise those three powers, that of enacting laws, that of executing the public resolutions, and that of judging the crimes or differences of individuals.

Most kingdoms of Europe enjoy a moderate government, because the prince, who is invested with the two first powers, leaves the third to his subjects. In Turky, where these three powers are united in the sultan's person, the subjects groan under the weight of a most frightful oppression.

In the republics of Italy, where these three powers are united, there is less liberty than in our monarchies. Hence their government is obliged to have recourse to as violent methods for its support, as even that of the Turks; witness the state-inquisitors,[6] and the lion's mouth into which every informer may at all hours throw his written accusations.

What a situation must the poor subject be in, under those republics! The same body of magistrates are possessed, as executors of the laws, of the whole power they have given themselves in quality of legislators. They may plunder the state by their general determinations; and as they have likewise the judiciary power in their hands, every private citizen may be ruined by their particular decisions.

The whole power is here united in one body; and though there is no external pomp that indicates a despotic sway, yet the people feel the effects of it every moment.

Hence it is that many of the princes of Europe, whose aim has been levelled at arbitrary power, have constantly set out with uniting in their own persons, all the branches of magistracy, and all the great offices of state.

I allow indeed that the mere hereditary aristocracy of the Italian republics, does not answer exactly to the despotic power of the eastern princes. The number of magistrates sometimes softens the power of the magistracy; the whole body of the nobles do not always concur in the same designs; and different tribunals are erected, that temper each other. Thus at Venice the legislative power is in the council, the executive in the pregadi, and the judiciary in the quarantia. But the mischief is, that these different tribunals are composed of magistrates all belonging to the same body; which constitutes almost one and the same power.

The judiciary power ought not be given to a standing senate; it should be exercised by persons taken from the body of the people,[7] at certain times of the year, and pursuant to a form and manner prescribed by law, in order to erect a tribunal that should last only as long as necessity requires.

By this means the power of judging, a power so terrible to mankind, not being annexed to any particular state or profession, becomes, as it were, invisible. People have not then the judges continually present to their view; they fear the office, but not the magistrate.

In accusations of a deep or criminal nature, it is proper the person accused should have the privilege of chusing in some measure his judges in concurrence with the law; or at least he should have a right to except against so great a number, that the remaining part may be deemed his own choice.

The other two powers may be given rather to magistrates or permanent bodies, because they are not exercised on any private subject; one being no more than the general will of the state, and the other the execution of that general will.

But though the tribunals ought not to be fixed, yet the judgments ought, and to such a degree as to be always conformable to the exact letter of the law. Were they to be the private opinion of the judge, people would then live in society without knowing exactly the obligations it lays them under.

The judges ought likewise to be in the same station as the accused, or, in other words, his peers, to the end that he may not imagine he is fallen into the hands of persons inclined to treat him with rigour.

If the legislature leaves the executive power in possession of a right to imprison those subjects who can give security for their good behaviour, there is an end of liberty; unless they are taken up, in order to answer without delay to a capital crime; in this case they are usually free, being subject only to the power of the law.

But should the legislature think itself in danger by some secret conspiracy against the state, or by a correspondence with a foreign enemy, it might authorise the executive power, for a short and limited time, to imprison suspected persons, who in that case would lose their liberty only for a while, to preserve it for ever.

And this is the only reasonable method, that can be substituted to the tyrannical magistracy of the Ephori, and to the state-inquisitors of Venice, who are also despotical.

As in a free state, every man who is supposed a free agent, ought to be his own governour; so the legislative power should reside in the whole body of the people. But since this is impossible in large states, and in small ones is subject to many inconveniencies; it is fit the people should act by their representatives, what they cannot act by themselves.

The inhabitants of a particular town are much better acquainted with its wants and interests, than with those of other places; and are better judges of the capacity of their neighbours, than of that of the rest of their countrymen. The members therefore of the legislature should not be chosen from the general body of the nation; but it is proper, that, in every considerable place, a representative should be elected by the inhabitants.

The great advantage of representatives is their being capable of discussing affairs. For this the people collectively are extremely unfit, which is one of the greatest inconveniencies of a democracy.

It is not at all necessary, that the representatives who have received a general instruction from their electors, should wait to be particularly instructed on every affair, as is practised in the diets of Germany. True it is, that, by this way of proceeding, the speeches of the deputies might with greater propriety be called the voice of the nation: But, on the other hand, this would throw them into infinite delays, would give each deputy a power of controlling the assembly; and, on the most urgent and pressing occasions, the springs of the nation might be stopped by a single caprice.

When the deputies, as Mr. Sidney well observes, represent a body of people, as in Holland, they ought to be accountable to their constituents: But it is a different thing in England, where they are deputed by boroughs.

All the inhabitants of the several districts ought to have a right of voting at the election of a representative, except such as are in so mean a situation, as to be deemed to have no will of their own.

One great fault there was in most of the ancient republics; that the people had a right to active resolutions, such as require some execution, a thing of which they are absolutely incapable, they ought to have no hand in the government, but for the chusing of representatives, which is within their reach. For though few can tell the exact degree of mens capacities, yet there are none but are capable of knowing in general whether the person they chuse is better qualified than most of his neighbours.

Neither ought the representative body to be chosen for active resolutions, for which it is not so fit; but for the enacting of laws, or to see whether the laws already enacted be duly executed, a thing they are very capable of, and which none indeed but themselves can properly perform.

In a state there are always persons distinguished by their birth, riches, or honours: But were they to be confounded with the common people, and to have only the weight of a single vote like the rest, the common liberty would be their slavery, and they would have no interest in supporting it, as most of the popular resolutions would be against them. The share they have therefore in the legislature ought to be proportioned to the other advantages they have in the state; which happens only when they form a body that has a right to put a stop to the enterprises of the people, as the people have a right to put a stop to theirs.

The legislative power is therefore committed to the body of the nobles, and to the body chosen to represent the people, which have each their assemblies and deliberations apart, each their separate views and interests.

Of the three powers above mentioned, the judicial is in some measure next to nothing. There remains therefore only two; and as these have need of a regulating power to temper them, the part of the legislative body composed of the nobility, is extremely proper for this very purpose.

The body of the nobility ought to be hereditary. In the first place, it is so in its own nature; and in the next, there must be a considerable interest to preserve its privileges; privileges that in themselves are obnoxious to popular envy, and of course, in a free state, are always in danger.

But as an hereditary power might be tempted to pursue its own particular interests, and forget those of the people; it is proper that where they may reap a singular advantage from being corrupted, as in the laws relating to the supplies, they should have no other share in the legislation, than the power of rejecting, and not that of resolving.

By the *power of resolving*, I mean the right of ordaining by their own authority, or of amending what has been ordained by others. By the *power of rejecting*, I would be understood to mean the right of annulling a resolution taken by another; which was the power of the tribunes at Rome.

And though the person possessed of the privilege of rejecting may likewise have the right of approving, yet this approbation passes for no more than a declaration, that he intends to make no use of his privilege of rejecting, and is derived from that very privilege.

The executive power ought to be in the hands of a monarch; because this branch of government, which has always need of expedition, is better administered by one than by many: Whereas, whatever depends on the legislative power, is oftentimes better regulated by many than by a single person.

But if there was no monarch, and the executive power was committed to a certain number of persons selected from the legislative body, there would be an end then of liberty; by reason the two powers would be united, as the same persons would actually sometimes have, and would moreover be always able to have, a share in both.

Were the legislative body to be a considerable time without meeting, this would likewise put an end to liberty. For one of these two things would naturally follow; either that there would be no longer any legislative resolutions, and then the state would fall into anarchy; or that these resolutions would be taken by the executive power, which would render it absolute.

It would be needless for the legislative body to continue always assembled. This would be troublesome to the representatives, and moreover would cut out too much work for the executive power, so as to take off its attention from executing, and oblige it to think only of defending its own prerogatives, and the right it has to execute.

Again, were the legislative body to be always assembled, it might happen to be kept up only by filling the places of the deceased members with new representatives; and in that case, if the legislative body was once corrupted, the evil would be past all remedy. When different legislative bodies succeed one another, the people who have a bad opinion of that which is actually sitting, may reasonably entertain some hopes of the next: But were it to be always the same body, the people, upon seeing it once corrupted, would no longer expect any good from its laws; and of course they would either become desperate, or fall into a state of indolence.

The legislative body should not assemble of itself. For a body is supposed to have no will but when it is assembled; and besides, were it not to assemble unanimously, it would be impossible to determine which was really the legislative body, the part assembled, or the other. And if it had a right to prorogue itself, it might happen never to be prorogued; which would be extremely dangerous, in case it should ever attempt to incroach on the executive power. Besides, there are seasons, some of which are more proper than others, for assembling the legislative body: It is fit therefore that the executive power should regulate the time of convening, as well as the duration of those assemblies, according to the circumstances and exigencies of state known to itself.

Were the executive power not to have a right of putting a stop to the incroachments of the legislative body, the latter would become despotic; for as it might arrogate to itself what authority it pleased, it would soon destroy all the other powers.

But it is not proper, on the other hand, that the legislative power should have a right to stop the executive. For as the execution has its natural limits, it is useless to confine it; besides, the executive power is generally employed in momentary operations. The power therefore of the Roman tribunes was faulty, as it put a stop not only to the legislation, but likewise to the execution itself; which was attended with infinite mischiefs.

But if the legislative power in a free government ought to have no right to stop the executive, it has a right, and ought to have the means of examining in what manner its laws have been executed; an advantage which this government has over that of Crete and Sparta, where the Cosmi and the Ephori gave no account of their administration.

But whatever may be the issue of that examination, the legislative body ought not to have a power of judging the person, nor of course the conduct of him who is intrusted with the executive power. His person should be sacred, because as it is necessary for the good of the state to prevent the legislative body from rendering themselves arbitrary, the moment he is accused or tried, there is an end of liberty.

In this case the state would be no longer a monarchy, but a kind of republican, though not a free government. But as the person intrusted with the executive power cannot abuse it without bad counsellors, and such as hate the laws as ministers, tho' the laws favour them as subjects; these men may be examined and punished. An advantage which this government has over that of Gnidus, where the law allowed of no such thing as calling the Amymenes[8] to an account, even after their administration;[9] and therefore the people could never obtain any satisfaction for the injuries done them.

Though in general the judiciary power ought not to be united with any part of the legislative, yet this is liable to three exceptions, founded on the particular interest of the party accused.

The great are always obnoxious to popular envy; and were they to be judged by the people, they might be in danger from their judges, and would moreover be deprived of the privilege which the meanest subject is possessed of in a free state, of being tried by their peers. The nobility for this reason ought not to be cited before the ordinary courts of judicature, but before that part of the legislature which is composed of their own body.

It is possible that the law, which is clear-sighted in one sense, and blind in another, might in some cases be too severe. But, as we have already observed, the national judges are no more than the mouth that pronounces the words of the law, mere passive beings, incapable of moderating either its force or rigour. That part therefore of the legislative body, which we have just now observed to be a necessary tribunal on another occasion, is also a necessary tribunal in this; it belongs to its supreme authority to moderate the law in favour of the law itself, by mitigating the sentence.

It might also happen that a subject intrusted with the administration of public affairs, might infringe the rights of the people, and be guilty of crimes which the ordinary magistrates either could not, or would not punish. But in general the legislative power cannot judge; and much less can it be a judge in this particular case, where it represents the party concerned, which is the people. It can only therefore impeach. But before what court shall it bring its impeachment? Must it go and abase itself before the ordinary tribunals, which are its inferiours, and being composed moreover of men who are chosen from the people as well as itself, will naturally be swayed by the authority of so powerful an accuser? No: In order to preserve the dignity of the people, and the security of the subject, the legislative part, which represents the people, must bring in its charge before the legislative part which represents the nobility, who have neither the same interests nor the same passions.

Here is an advantage which this government has over most of the ancient republics, where there was this abuse, that the people were at the same time both judge and accuser.

The executive power, pursuant to what has been already said, ought to have a share in the legislature by the power of rejecting, otherwise it would soon be stripped of its prerogative. But should the legislative power usurp a share of the executive, the latter would be equally undone.

If the prince were to have a share in the legislature by the power of resolving, liberty would be lost. But as it is necessary he should have a share in the legislature for the support of his own prerogative, this share must consist in the power of rejecting.

The change of government at Rome was owing to this, that neither the senate, who had one part of the executive power, nor the magistrates, who were intrusted with the other, had the right of rejecting, which was entirely lodged in the people.

Here then is the fundamental constitution of the government we are treating of. The legislative body being composed of two parts, one checks the other, by the mutual privilege of rejecting. They are both checked by the executive power, as the executive is by the legislative.

These three powers should naturally form a state of repose or inaction. But as there is a necessity for movement in the course of human affairs, they are forced to move, but still to move in concert.

As the executive power has no other part in the legislative than the privilege of rejecting, it can have no share in the public debates. It is not even necessary that it should propose, because as it may always disapprove of the resolutions that shall be taken, it may likewise reject the decisions on those proposals which were made against its will.

In some ancient commonwealths, where public debates were carried on by the people in a body, it was natural for the executive power to propose and debate with the people, otherwise their resolutions must have been attended with a strange confusion.

Were the executive power to ordain the raising of public money, otherwise than by giving its consent, liberty would be at an end; because it would become legislative in the most important point of legislation.

If the legislative power was to settle the subsidies, not from year to year, but for ever, it would run the risk of losing its liberty, because the executive power would no longer be dependent; and when once it was possessed of such a perpetual right, it would be a matter of indifference, whether it held of itself, or of another. The same may be said if it should fix, not from year to year, but for ever, the sea and land forces with which it is to intrust the executive power.

To prevent the executive power from being able to oppress, it is requisite, that the armies, with which it is intrusted, should consist of the people, and have the same spirit as the people, as was the case at Rome, till the time of Marius. To obtain this end, there are only two ways, either that the persons employed in the army should have sufficient property to answer for their conduct to their fellow-subjects, and be inlisted only for a year, as was customary at Rome: Or if there should be a standing army, composed chiefly of the most despicable part of the nation, the legislative power should have a right to disband them as soon as it pleased; the soldiers should live in common with the rest of the people; and no separate camp, barracks, or fortress, should be suffered.

When once an army is established, it ought not to depend immediately on the legislative, but on the executive power; and this from the very nature of the thing; its business consisting more in action than in deliberation.

From a manner of thinking that prevails amongst mankind, they set a higher value upon courage than timorousness, on activity than prudence, on strength than counsel. Hence the army will ever despise a senate, and respect their own officers. They will naturally slight the orders sent them by a body of men, whom they look upon as cowards, and therefore unworthy to command them. So that as soon as the army depends on the legislative body, the government becomes a military one; and if the contrary has ever happened, it has been owing to some extraordinary circumstances. It is because the army was always kept divided; it is because it was composed of several bodies, that depended each on their particular province; it is because the capital towns were strong places, defended by their natural situation, and not garrisoned with regular troops. Holland, for instance, is still safer than Venice; she might drown, or starve the revolted troops; for as they are not quartered in towns capable of furnishing them with necessary subsistence, this subsistence is of course precarious.

Whoever shall read the admirable treatise of Tacitus on the manners of the Germans,[10] will find that it is from them the English have borrowed the idea of their political government. This beautiful system was invented first in the woods.

As all human things have an end, the state we are speaking of will lose its liberty, it will perish. Have not Rome, Sparta and Carthage perished? It will perish when the legislative power shall be more corrupted than the executive.

It is not my business to examine whether the English actually enjoy this liberty, or not. It is sufficient for my purpose to observe, that it is established by their laws; and I inquire no further.

Neither do I pretend by this to undervalue other governments, nor to say that this extreme political liberty ought to give uneasiness to those who have only a moderate share of it. How should I have any such design, I who think that even the excess of reason is not always desirable, and that mankind generally find their account better in mediums than in extremes?

Montesquieu's Notes

1. I have copied, says Cicero, Scevola's edict, which permits the Greeks to terminate their differences among themselves according to their own laws, this makes them consider themselves as a free people.

2. The Russians could not bear that the Czar Peter should make them cut it off.

3. The Cappadocians refused the condition of a republican state, which was offered them by the Romans.

4. The natural end of a state that has no foreign enemies, or that thinks itself secured against them by barriers.

5. Inconveniency of the *liberum veto*.

6. At Venice.

7. As at Athens.

8. These were magistrates chosen annually by the people. See Stephen of Byzantium.

9. It was lawful to accuse the Roman magistrates after the expiration of their several offices. See in Dionys Halicarn 1.9 the affair of Genucius the tribune.

10. De minoribus rebus principes consultant, de majoribus omnes; in tamen ut ea quoque, quorum penes plebem arbitrium est, apud principes pertractentur.

James Madison: The Federalist (1788)

Copies of *The Spirit of Laws* were in many eighteenth-century libraries, and numerous newspaper advertisements offered it for sale to colonial book collectors. Montesquieu's writings were widely dispersed among the colonial population. The most obvious example of his practical effect is in the U.S. Constitution, with its elaborate provisions for a checks-and-balances system, but historians have disagreed on the degree to which Montesquieu influenced the men at Philadelphia. Some have argued that the factor which shaped the Constitution was colonial experience and denied Montesquieu any significance at all. The truth probably lies somewhere in between these two points of view.

There can be no doubt, however, about Montesquieu's influence upon the following selection from *The Federalist Papers*. Madison, Hamilton, and Jay collaborated on this series of newspaper articles designed to persuade the people of New York to support ratification of the new Constitution. In this excerpt from *The Federalist No. 47*, Madison defends the convention's work from the anti-Federalists' charge that it violated Montesquieu's doctrine of the separation of powers.

To the People of the State of New York:

Having reviewed the general form of the proposed government and the general mass of power allotted to it, I proceed to examine the particular structure of this government, and the distribution of this mass of power among its constituent parts.

One of the principal objections inculcated by the more respectable adversaries to the Constitution, is its supposed violation of the political maxim, that the legislative, executive, and judiciary departments ought to be separate and distinct. In the structure of the federal government, no regard, it is said, seems to have been paid to this essential precaution in favor of liberty. The several departments of power are distributed and blended in such a manner as at once to destroy all symmetry and beauty of form, and to expose some of the essential parts of the edifice to the dangers of being crushed by the disproportionate weight of other parts.

From *The Federalist, on the New Constitution written in the year 1788* . . . (Hallowell, Me.: Glazier & Co., 1826), pp. 270–73.

No political truth is certainly of greater intrinsic value, or is stamped with the authority of more enlightened patrons of liberty, than that on which the objection is founded. The accumulation of all powers, legislative, executive, and judiciary, in the same hands, whether of one, a few, or many, and whether hereditary, self-appointed, or elective, may justly be pronounced the very definition of tyranny. Were the federal Constitution, therefore, really chargeable with the accumulation of power, or with a mixture of powers, having a dangerous tendency to such an accumulation, no further arguments would be necessary to inspire a universal reprobation of the system. I persuade myself, however, that it will be made apparent to every one, that the charge cannot be supported, and that the maxim on which it relies has been totally misconceived and misapplied. In order to form correct ideas on this important subject, it will be proper to investigate the sense in which the preservation of liberty requires that the three great departments of power should be separate and distinct.

The oracle who is always consulted and cited on this subject is the celebrated Montesquieu. If he be not the author of this invaluable precept in the science of politics, he has the merit at least of displaying and recommending it most effectually to the attention of mankind. Let us endeavor, in the first place, to ascertain his meaning on this point.

The British Constitution was to Montesquieu what Homer has been to the didactic writers on epic poetry. As the latter have considered the work of the immortal bard as the perfect model from which the principles and rules of the epic art were to be drawn, and by which all similar works were to be judged, so this great political critic appears to have viewed the Constitution of England as the standard, or to use his own expression, as the mirror of political liberty; and to have delivered, in the form of elementary truths, the several characteristic principles of that particular system. That we may be sure, then, not to mistake his meaning in this case, let us recur to the source from which the maxim was drawn.

On the slightest view of the British Constitution, we must perceive that the legislative, executive, and judiciary departments are by no means totally separate and distinct from each other. The executive magistrate forms an integral part of the legislative authority. He alone has the prerogative of making treaties with foreign sovereigns, which, when made, have, under certain limitations, the force of legislative acts. All the members of the judiciary department are appointed by him, can be removed by him on the address of the two Houses of Parliament, and form, when he pleases to consult them, one of his constitutional councils. One branch of the legislative department forms also a great constitutional council to the executive chief, as, on another hand, it is the sole depositary of judicial power in cases of impeachment, and is invested with the supreme appellate jurisdiction in all other cases. The judges, again, are so far connected with the legislative department as often to attend and participate in its deliberations, though not admitted to a legislative vote.

From these facts, by which Montesquieu was guided, it may clearly be inferred that, in saying "There can be no liberty where the legislative and executive powers are united in the same person, or body of magistrates," or, "if the power of judging be not separated from the legislative and executive powers," he did not mean that these departments ought to have no *partial agency* in, or no *control* over, the acts of each other. His meaning, as his own words import, and still more conclusively as illustrated by the example in his eye, can amount to no more than this, that where the *whole* power of one department is exercised by the same hands which possess the *whole* power of another department, the fundamental principles of a free constitution are subverted. This would have been the case in the constitution examined by him if the king, who is the sole executive magistrate, had possessed also the complete legislative power, or the supreme administration of justice; or if the entire legislative body had possessed the supreme judiciary, or the supreme executive authority. This, however, is not among the vices of that constitution. The magistrate in whom the whole executive power resides cannot of himself make a law, though he can put a negative on every law; nor administer justice in person, though he has the appointment of those who do administer it. The judges can exercise no executive prerogative, though they are shoots from the executive stock; nor any legislative function, though they may be advised with by the legislative councils. The entire legislature can perform no judiciary act, though by the joint act of two of its branches the judges may be removed from their offices, and though one of its branches is possessed of the judicial power in the last resort. The entire legislature, again, can

exercise no executive prerogative, though one of its branches constitutes the supreme executive magistracy, and another, on the impeachment of a third, can try and condemn all the subordinate
officers in the executive department.

The reasons on which Montesquieu grounds his maxim are a
further demonstration of his meaning. "When the legislative and
executive powers are united in the same person or body," says he,
"there can be no liberty, because apprehensions may arise lest *the
same* monarch or senate should *enact* tyrannical laws to *execute*
them in a tyrannical manner." Again: "Were the power of judging
joined with the legislative, the life and liberty of the subject would
be exposed to arbitrary control, for *the judge* would then be *the
legislator.* Were it joined to the executive power, *the judge* might
behave with all the violence of *an oppressor.*" Some of these
reasons are more fully explained in other passages; but briefly
stated as they are here, they suffiiciently establish the meaning
which we have put on this celebrated maxim of this celebrated
author.

If we look into the constitutions of the several States, we find
that, notwithstanding the emphatical and, in some instances, the
unqualified terms in which this axiom has been laid down, there
is not a single instance in which the several departments of power
have been kept absolutely separate and distinct. . . .

Chapter VI

William Blackstone (1723-80)

What Montesquieu attempted to do for political theory, Sir William Blackstone tried to do for the English legal system: make it appear a part of one harmonious universal system. The English common law was the product of centuries of custom, practice, and tradition. Unlike the civil law, which rested upon Justinian's Code, the common law had no codifiers; students examined it through the series of commentaries produced by famous English jurists. Arising out of feudalism, the common law had become the tool which Englishmen used to thwart their monarchs' pretensions to absolutism. Early in the seventeenth century Sir Edward Coke had invoked the common law in an attempt to refute the divine-right philosophy of James I. Throughout the Restoration period, Whigs tried to reestablish the medieval principle that the king was under the law.

The Glorious Revolution and the subsequent Acts of Settlement accomplished that aim.

The common law was a subject of some interest then to Englishmen, but the English universities did not teach courses in it; their only law courses dealt with the Roman-derived civil law, which was of limited application to domestic concerns. In 1756 William Blackstone, graduate of Oxford, fellow of All Souls College, student of both civil and common law, was an unsuccessful practicing lawyer.

He had recently been disappointed in his hopes of preferment when the Duke of Newcastle passed him over in appointing a new professor of civil law at Oxford. On the urging of a friend, however, he began to read lectures on the common law at his college. Quickly they became very popular, both because of the felicity of Blackstone's style and because of the topic's newness to undergraduates. His college soon formalized his educational activities by creating the first chair of English law in the English universities and appointing Blackstone to fill it.

As his fame spread, illicit copies of his lectures appeared, and Blackstone, determined to cash in on this market, began composition of a general survey of the English law. In 1765 the first volume of the *Commentaries* appeared, followed by three more volumes in the next four years. In his anxiety to make the law seem part of one harmonious whole, Blackstone slurred over many of its inconsistencies, opening the way for criticism by more scholarly jurists. Nevertheless, the readability of his work recommended it to laymen, and by the end of the century it had become the authoritative textbook for students.

Commentaries on the Laws of England (1765)

The Nature of Laws in General

Defined.   In its broadest sense, law signifies a rule of action. It embraces all kinds of actions, animate or inanimate, rational and irrational. Thus we say: the laws of motion, of gravitation, of optics, of mechanics, as well as the laws of nature and of nations. It is that rule of action, which is prescribed by some superior, and which the inferior is bound to obey.

Fixed Principles.   At the creation of matter, God impressed certain principles upon it, from which it can never depart, and without which it would cease to be. He then established certain laws of motion, to which all movable bodies must conform. So a clockmaker establishes certain arbitrary laws for the movements of the time-piece, following which it answers the end of its formation.

From William Blackstone, *Commentaries on the Laws of England,* ed. William Hardcastle Browne (New York: L. K. Strauss, 1892), pp. 7–8, 37–44.

Natural Law. The same rule holds as to vegetable and animal life, which are governed by fixed laws. The progress of plants from the seed to the root, and from thence to the seed again; the method of animal nutrition, digestion, secretion and other branches of vital economy are not left to chance or to the will of the creature itself, but are guided by unerring rules laid down by the Creator.

Human Law. Laws, in the confined sense we shall treat of them, denote the rules not of action in general, but of human action, that is, the precepts by which man must regulate his behavior.

Divine Law. The will of his Maker is called the law of nature. Man is entirely a dependent being, subject to the laws of his Creator, to whose will he must conform. Although endowed with free will, yet it is regulated and restrained in some degree by certain immutable laws of good and evil, to which Deity Himself conforms. These principles are included among others, that we should live honestly, should hurt no one, and should render to every one his due. To these three precepts, Justinian has reduced the whole doctrine of law. As a Being of infinite power He could prescribe any laws, however unjust and severe, but as a Being also of infinite wisdom, He has laid down only such laws, as are based upon justice.

Divine Goodness. As a Being of infinite goodness, God has so inseparably connected the laws of eternal justice with the happiness of each individual, that the latter cannot be attained, without observing the former. He has graciously reduced the rule of obedience to this one precept, that man should pursue his own true and substantial happiness. This is the foundation of ethics or natural law.

Law of Nature. This law, being coeval with mankind and dictated by God Himself, is obligatory upon all. No human laws are of any validity if contrary to this, as they derive their force and authority from this original. We must discover what the law of nature directs in every circumstance of life, by considering what method will tend the most effectually to our own substantial happiness.

Revealed Divine Law. In compassion for the imperfections of human reason, God has mercifully at times discovered and enforced His laws by direct revelations. These are found in the holy scriptures. These precepts, when revealed, are really a part of the original law of nature. The revealed law is of greater authenticity, than the moral system framed by ethical writers, termed the natural law, because one is the law of nature, as declared to be by God Himself; the other is only what, by the light of human reason, we imagine to be that law.

Foundation of Human Law.   Upon these two foundations, the law of nature and the law of revelation, depend all human laws; *i.e.* no human laws should contradict them. Upon indifferent points, the divine and natural law leave a man at his own liberty, subject for the benefit of society to restraint within certain limits. With regard to points that are not indifferent, human laws are only declaratory of and in subordination to the divine law.

Example. Instance of Murder.   This crime is expressly forbidden by the divine law, and demonstrably by the natural law, and from these prohibitions arise the true unlawfulness of the crime. Those human laws that annex a punishment to it do not increase its moral guilt. If, therefore, any human law should allow or enjoin the commission of such crime, we should disobey such law, or we would offend both the natural and divine.

The Rights of Persons

Defined.   The rights of persons, as commanded by the municipal law, are of two sorts: first, such as are due from every citizen, which are usually called civil duties; and secondly, such as belong to him, which is the more popular acceptation of right or *jura.* Both may indeed be comprised in this latter division, but it will be more clear to consider them as duties acquired from, rather than as rights belonging to particular persons.

Division of Persons.   Persons are divided by law into either natural or artificial. Natural persons are such as the God of nature formed us; artificial are such as are created and devised by human laws, for the purposes of society and government, and are called corporations or bodies politic.

Division of Rights.   The rights of persons, considered in their natural capacities, are also of two sorts, absolute and relative. Absolute, which are such as appertain to particular men, merely as individuals or single persons; relative, which are incident to them as members of society, and standing in various relations to each other.

Absolute Rights of Individuals

Defined.   By absolute rights, are meant those which are so in their primary and strictest sense; such as would belong to their persons merely in a state of nature, and which every man is entitled to enjoy, whether out of society or in it.

Absolute Duties.   But with regard to the absolute duties which man is bound to perform, considered as a mere individual, it is not to be expected, that any municipal law should at all explain or enforce them. For the end and intent of such laws being only to regulate the behavior of mankind, as they are members of society, and stand in various relations to each other, they have consequently no concern with any but social or relative duties. No matter how abandoned may be a man's principles, or how vicious his practice, provided he keeps his wickedness to himself, and does not violate public decency, he is out of the reach of human laws. But if he makes his vices public, then they become by his bad example, of pernicious effect to society, and it is the business of human laws to correct them.

Rights and Duties Distinguished.   But with respect to rights, the case is different. Human laws define and enforce, as well those rights which belong to a man as an individual, as those which belong to him as related to others.

Primary Aim of Law.   The principal aim of society is to protect individuals in the enjoyment of those absolute rights, which were vested in them by the immutable laws of nature, but which could not be preserved in peace, without the mutual assistance and intercourse of social communities. The primary end of human laws is to maintain and regulate these absolute rights of individuals. Such rights as are social and relative, result from the formation of states and societies, so that to maintain them is clearly a subsequent consideration. Therefore the principal object of human laws should be to explain, protect and enforce such rights as are absolute, which in themselves are few and simple, and then such rights as are relative, which are numerous and complicated.

Natural Liberty.   The absolute rights of man, considered as a free agent, are denominated the natural liberty of mankind, which consists in a power of acting, as one thinks fit, without any restraint or control, unless by the law of nature; being a right inherent in us by birth, when God endowed man with free will. But every man, when he enters into society, gives up a part of his natural liberty, as the price of so valuable a boon, and obliges himself to conform to those laws, which the community has thought proper to establish. Otherwise there would be no security to individuals in any of the enjoyments of life.

Civil Liberty. Political or civil liberty is no other than natural liberty, so far restrained by human laws, as is requisite for the general advantage of the public. The law which restrains a man from doing mischief to his fellow citizens, though it diminishes the natural, increases the civil liberty of mankind; but every causeless restraint of the will of the subject is a degree of tyranny, and even laws themselves, if they regulate our conduct in matters of mere indifference, are destructive of liberty. That constitution or frame of government, that system of laws, is alone calculated to maintain civil liberty, which leaves the subject master of his own conduct, except in those points, wherein the public good requires some direction or restraint. Locke has well said: "Where there is no law, there is no freedom." The idea and practice of this political or civil liberty flourish in their highest vigor in these kingdoms, and can only be lost by the folly or demerits of its owner. They are founded on nature and reason, and are coeval with the English form of government, though subject at times to fluctuations and change. From time to time, their fundamental articles have been asserted in parliament, as often as they were thought to be in danger.

Magna Carta. This great charter of liberty was obtained by force from king John, and afterwards was confirmed by his son Henry III. It contained but few new grants, but was for the most part declaratory of the fundamental laws of England. A statute subsequently directed this charter to be allowed, as the common law, and all judgments contrary to it were declared void.

Different Acts of Parliament. Then followed corroborating statutes from Edward I to Henry IV. After a long interval, appeared the Petition of Right, assented to by Charles I, in the beginning of his reign, which was a parliamentary declaration of the liberties of the people. More ample concessions were subsequently made by this unhappy prince to his parliament. Then came the famous *Habeas Corpus* act under Charles II. To these succeeded the Bill of Rights, delivered by the lords and commons to William and Mary, on their accession to the throne in 1688. Lastly these liberties were again asserted at the commencement of the eighteenth century in the Act of Settlement, whereby the succession to the crown was limited to the house then in power.

Of What the Rights Consist. The rights themselves, thus defined by these several statutes, consist in a number of private immunities, the residuum of natural liberty, which was not required to be sacrificed by the laws of society to public convenience, or else those civil privileges, which society had engaged to provide, in lieu of the natural liberties, so given up by individuals.

Division of Rights. These may be reduced to three principal or primary articles:

1. *The right of personal security.*
2. *The right of personal liberty.*
3. *The right of private property.*

Right of Personal Security

Defined. This right consists in a person's legal and uninterrupted enjoyment of his life, his limbs, his body, his health and his reputation.

1. Life. This right is inherent by nature in every individual, and exists even before the child is actually born.

Rights of Unborn Child. The offence of abortion of a quick child is not murder, but homicide or manslaughter. An infant *in ventre sa mere* is supposed in law to be born for many purposes. It is capable of having a legacy made to it. It may have a guardian assigned to it, and may have an estate limited to its use, and to take afterwards by such limitation, as if it were then actually born. The same ruling holds in the civil law.

2. Limbs. Such limbs as are referred to here, are those members which may be useful to a man in fight, and the loss of which alone amounts to *mayhem* in the common law. By the possession of these, he can protect himself from external injuries, and they cannot be destroyed or disabled, without a manifest breach of civil liberty. Homicide even is pardonable, if done in self defense of life or limb. And the same is a sufficient excuse for the commission of many misdemeanors.

Duress. The constraint a man is under in these circumstances is termed duress, from the Latin *durities,* of which there are two sorts, duress of imprisonment, where a man loses his liberty, and duress *per minas,* where the hardship is only threatened. Duress *per minas* is either for fear of loss of life, or else for fear of mayhem or loss of limb. And this fear must be upon sufficient reason. A fear of battery or being beaten is no duress, nor of having one's house burned, or of goods taken away or destroyed, because in such cases, a man may have satisfaction in equivalent damages, but no suitable atonement can be made for the loss of life or limb.

Relief of the Poor. The law not only regards life and limb, but furnishes a man with everything necessary to his support. No man is so poor, but he may demand a supply sufficient for all the necessities of life from the more opulent, by the several statutes ordained for the relief of the poor.

Civil Death. These rights can only be terminated by the death of the person, by a civil or natural death. The civil death commenced, if a man was banished the realm by the process of the common law, or entered into a monastery and became a professed monk, in which cases he was absolutely dead in law, and his heir took his estate. A monk, on taking his vows, was deemed *civiliter mortuus*, and like other dying men might make his will and appoint executors, or the ordinary in case of his intestacy, might grant letters of administration to his next of kin. Even a lease made to a third person during the life of one, who afterwards became a monk, terminated by his entry into a monastery. Hence the use of the term "natural life" in legal documents. No cognizance was taken in England of vows made in a foreign country. This disability has been abolished, and also that of banishment, consequent upon abjuration.

Natural Death. The natural life, the gift of the Creator, cannot legally be destroyed by an individual, neither by the person himself, nor by any class of individuals, merely on their own authority. Yet it may be forfeited for the breach of those laws of society, which are enforced by the sanction of capital punishment. The statute law of England very seldom, and the common law never inflicts any punishment extending to life or limb, unless upon the highest necessity, and under the express warrant of law.

3. *Body.* The remainder of a man's body or person is also entitled, by the same natural right, to security from the corporal insults of menaces, assaults, beating and wounding.

4. *Health.* A man's health is entitled to preservation from such practices, as may prejudice or annoy.

5. *Reputation.* The security of his reputation or good name from the venom of detraction and slander, is a right to which every

man is entitled by reason and natural justice, for without these, it is impossible to have the perfect enjoyment of any other advantage or right.

Right of Personal Liberty

Defined.   This consists in the power of locomotion, of changing situation, or moving one's person to whatever place one's own inclination may direct, without imprisonment or restraint, unless by due course of law. It is a right strictly natural, which the laws of England have never abridged without sufficient cause, and which cannot be abridged by a magistrate, without the explicit permission of the laws. No freeman shall be imprisoned or detained without cause shown, to which he may make answer according to law.

Habeas Corpus Act.   By this act, passed in the reign of Charles II, no subject of England can be long detained in prison, except in those cases, in which the law requires and justifies such detainer. Lest this act be evaded by demanding unreasonable bail or sureties, a later act enacts, that excessive bail shall not be required. It is only in cases of great emergency to the state, that the operations of this act are suspended for a limited time to imprison persons suspected of treason, without assigning cause therefor. In such cases as these, the nation parts with its liberty for the time, in order to preserve it forever.

Duress.   The confinement of the person is an imprisonment, so that the keeping a man against his will in a private house, arresting or forcibly detaining him, is an imprisonment. If a man is under duress of imprisonment, which is a compulsion by an illegal restraint of liberty, until he seals a document, or the like, he may allege the duress and avoid the extorted bond. But if a man be lawfully imprisoned, and either to procure his discharge or for other cause, seals a bond or deed, this is not by duress of imprisonment, and he cannot avoid it.

Process Must Be Regular.   To make imprisonment lawful, it must either be by process from the courts of judicature, or by warrant from some legal officer, having authority to commit, which warrant must be in writing, under the hand and seal of the magistrate, and express the causes of the commitment, in order to be examined into, if necessary, upon a *habeas corpus.* If there be no cause expressed, the jailer is not bound to detain the prisoner.

Ne Exeat.   A consequence of this personal liberty is, that every

Englishman may claim a right to abide in his own country, so long as he pleases, and not to be driven from it, unless by the sentence of the law. The king, by his royal prerogative, may issue his writ *ne exeat regnum*, and prohibit a subject leaving the country. This may be necessary for the public service.

Transportation and Exile.   But no power, except the authority of parliament, can send any subject of England out of the land against his will, not even if he be a criminal. Exile and transportation are unknown to the common law, and whenever the latter is now inflicted, it is either by the choice of the criminal himself to escape a capital punishment, or else by some express statute. *Magna carta* declares, that no freeman shall be banished, unless by the judgment of his peers or by the law of the land.

Violation of Habeas Corpus Act.   By the *habeas corpus* act, that second *magna carta*, and stable bulwark of our liberties, it is enacted, that no subject of the realm shall be sent as prisoner abroad, but that all such imprisonments shall be illegal. One who shall dare to commit another contrary to law, shall be disqualified from holding office, shall incur the penalty of a *praemunire* and be incapable of receiving pardon; and the party suffering shall also have his private action against the person committing, and shall recover treble costs, besides his damages, the minimum being five hundred pounds.

Expulsion Illegal.   Though within the realm, the king may command the attendance and service of all his liegemen, yet he cannot send any man out of the realm, even upon the public service, excepting sailors and soldiers, the nature of whose employment necessarily implies an exception.

Right of Private Property

Defined.   This is the third absolute right, and consists in the free use, enjoyment and disposal by a man of all his acquisitions, without any control or diminution, save only by the laws of the land. The original of private property is probably founded in nature.

Obligations to Society.   Its modifications, the method of preserving it in the present owner, and of transferring it from man to man, are entirely derived from society, and are some of the civil advantages, in exchange for which every individual has resigned a part of his natural liberty.

Unjust Seizure of Lands.   Upon this principle, the great charter has declared, that no freeman shall be disseised or divested of his freehold, or of his liberties or free customs, but by the judgment of his peers, or by the law of the land. By a variety of ancient statutes, it is enacted, that no man's lands or goods shall be seized into the king's hands, against the great charter and the law of the land, and that no man shall be disinherited, or expelled from his franchises or freehold, unless dispossessed by course of law.

Public Good Secondary.   The law will not authorize a violation of the right of property, even for the public good. Thus a new road through private grounds may be beneficial to the community, but it cannot be laid out without the consent of the owner of the land. In vain, may it be urged, that the good of the individual ought to yield to that of the community, for it would be dangerous to allow any private man, or even any public tribunal, to be judge of this common good, and to decide on its expediency. Besides the public good is interested in the protection of every individual's private rights, as modelled by the municipal law.

Eminent Domain.   In this and similar cases, the legislature alone can interpose, and compel the individual to acquiesce. It does this, not by arbitrarily depriving the party of his property, but by giving him a full indemnification and equivalent for the injury thereby sustained. The public is now considered as an individual, treating with an individual for an exchange. All that the legislature does, is to oblige the owner to alienate his possessions for a reasonable price, and even this is an exertion of power, which the legislature indulges with caution.

Taxes, How Levied.   Nor is this the only instance, in which the law of the land has postponed even public necessity to the sacred rights of private property. No subject can be constrained to pay any taxes, even for the support of government, but such as are imposed by his own consent or that of his representative in parliament. Under the petition of right of Charles I, no man shall be compelled to yield any tax without common consent, by act of parliament.

Nathaniel Chipman:
Sketches of the Principles of Government (1793)

Very shortly after its publication, Blackstone's *Commentaries* became the standard reference tool for colonial lawyers and courts. It enjoyed greater popularity in America than in England; colonial students avidly studied it. Even the Revolution failed to diminish its popularity, since the English common law became the basis of the American legal system. So popular was Blackstone that he drew the ire of many who believed the new nation required a native law, or who realized the shortcomings of Blackstone's interpretation of English law. Jefferson was one of those who felt that Blackstone's influence was making monarchists of young lawyers. Partly to answer such complaints, St. George Tucker, professor of law at William and Mary, produced an Americanized version of Blackstone in 1805. Thus in the early nineteenth century Blackstone remained the principal source of legal information in the United States.

The following selection is from a book by Nathaniel Chipman, a chief justice of the Vermont Supreme Court and a U.S. Senator. His *Sketches of the Principles of Government* (1793) was a discussion of the problems of developing a legal system for a new state and nation. Nationalist in his outlook, he, like Jefferson, feared the "foreign" influence of Blackstone. This excerpt is a call for an American Blackstone and testifies in a negative sense to Blackstone's pervasiveness in American culture.

> The governments of the several American states, as well as that of the Union, are of the democratic republican kind. We ought to know their principles, to study well their tendency, and to be able both in theory and practice to exclude all foreign principles.
>
> Judge Blackstone was a British subject, highly in favor with the government. He was enamoured with its principles. He has blazoned them with all his rhetoric, and not the least those, which are the most faulty. Probably to these, notwithstanding his great abilities, he was chiefly indebted for his pre-eminence. Unhappily, his Commentaries are the only treatise of law, to which the law students, in these states, have access. In every section of the criminal code, and no less, in every question of a civil nature, where the prerogative of the Crown, or the privilege of the Peers intervene, the principles of the British government have given a cast to his reasonings. I wish not to detract from the merit of the author, as a British subject; a writer who has, in a masterly manner, delineated the laws and jurisprudence of a foreign nation, under a government very different from our own.

From Nathaniel Chipman, *Sketches of the Principles of Government* (Rutland, Vt., from the press of J. Lyon, printed for the author, 1793), pp. 29–30.

There are many things in his Commentaries, which accord with the principles of the American governments, and which are founded in the universal principles of jurisprudence. These, however, will be found to be derived from the democratic part of the British constitution. The student should carefully learn to distinguish those principles, which are peculiar to that government, or governments of a similar constitution; to distinguish the reasonings, which are accommodated to those principles, or solely dictated by them. He ought to know, that they are not universal; that in a democratic republic, they are wholly inadmissible. This is not enough. He should be led through a system of laws applicable to our governments, and a train of reasoning congenial to their principles. Such a system we yet want. Surely genius is not wanting in America. Can none be found equal to the arduous, the important task? Perhaps, we are not yet fully ripe for the undertaking. Years may be necessary for its completion. But he who shall only prepare the rudiments, will deserve highly of his country.

Chapter VII

Adam Smith (1723-90)

Just as Montesquieu looked for a set of natural laws in politics, so others sought the natural laws of economics. The prevailing economic doctrine was mercantilism, which assumed that the measure of a nation's wealth was gold and silver and that government, by a conscious policy, could greatly facilitate the accumulation of natural wealth. It led to government's assuming a very active role in subsidizing and regulating economic activity. The English Acts of Trade and Navigation which restricted the commercial activities of the English colonies reflected mercantilist doctrine.

The first attack upon the doctrines of mercantilism came from a group of Frenchmen called physiocrats. Concerned by the stagnating state of French agriculture, François Quesnay (1694–1774), a court physician, and the Marquis de Mirabeau (1715–89) formulated the doctrine of *laissez-faire*, which called upon government to free agricultural entrepreneurs from restrictive taxation and allow the natural laws of the marketplace to operate. The physiocrats expressed a pronounced agrarian bias; they divided all of society into a productive class, which comprised those in agricultural pursuits, and a "sterile" class, which include all in manufacturing and commerce. Their thought helped shape the young Jefferson's ideas on the virtue of the yeoman farmer. Such a bias, however, had little appeal to a country such as England, just beginning to enter the industrial revolution.

It remained for the great Scottish philosopher Adam Smith (1723–90) to lead the attack upon British mercantilism and to lay the foundation of economic thought for a century to come. Educated in philosophy at the Universities of Glasgow and Oxford, he subsequently became a lecturer on logical and moral philosophy at Glasgow.

In 1761 a visit to London resulted in an appointment as a traveling tutor to the Duke of Buccleuch. Teacher and pupil set out for France, where Smith met many of the *philosophes*, including Quesnay. While abroad he resigned his chair at Glasgow, and upon returning to England he set to work upon his masterpiece, *An Inquiry into the Nature and Causes of the Wealth of Nations*, which appeared in 1776.

The question of Smith's indebtedness to the physiocrats is a matter of dispute, but his work clearly placed more importance upon the role of manufacturing and commerce than theirs. *Wealth of Nations* quickly attained a popularity unrivaled by any other work in the field—indeed, it helped found economics as a separate field of inquiry. It was influential in shaping the tax policies of the North administration during the American Revolution and was assiduously studied by William Pitt. A whole generation of Englishmen were to elaborate upon Smith to develop the "classical school" of economics.

The selections which follow comprise two sets: the first illustrates Smith's natural-law approach to the problems of the marketplace; the second is an attack upon the basic assumptions of mercantilism, concluding with a plea for *laissez-faire*.

Adam Smith: Wealth of Nations (1776)

Of the Natural and Market Price of Commodities

There is in every society or neighbourhood an ordinary or average rate both of wages and profit in every different employment of labour and stock. This rate is naturally regulated, as I shall show hereafter, partly by the general circumstances of the society, their riches or poverty, their advancing, stationary, or declining condition; and partly by the particular nature of each employment.

From Adam Smith, *An Inquiry into the Nature and Causes of the Wealth of Nations*, 11th ed. (London: T. Cadell & W. Davies, 1805), vol. I, pp. 84–90; vol. II, pp. 146–47, 160–62, 559–69; vol. III, pp. 42–43.

There is likewise in every society or neighbourhood an ordinary or average rate of rent, which is regulated too, as I shall show hereafter, partly by the general circumstances of the society or neighbourhood in which the land is situated, and partly by the natural or improved fertility of the land.

These ordinary or average rates may be called the natural rates of wages, profit, and rent, at the time and place in which they commonly prevail.

When the price of any commodity is neither more nor less than what is sufficient to pay the rent of the land, the wages of the labour, and the profits of the stock employed in raising, preparing, and bringing it to market, according to their natural rates, the commodity is then sold for what may be called its natural price.[1]

The commodity is then sold precisely for what it is worth, or for what it really costs the person who brings it to market; for though in common language what is called the prime cost of any commodity does not comprehend the profit of the person who is to sell it again, yet if he sells it at a price which does not allow him the ordinary rate of profit in his neighbourhood, he is evidently a loser by the trade; since by employing his stock in some other way he might have made that profit. His profit, besides, is his revenue, the proper fund of his subsistence. As, while he is preparing and bringing the goods to market, he advances to his workmen their wages, or their subsistence; so he advances to himself, in the same manner, his own subsistence, which is generally suitable to the profit which he may reasonably expect from the sale of his goods. Unless they yield him this profit, therefore, they do not repay him what they may very properly be said to have really cost him.

Though the price, therefore, which leaves him this profit, is not always the lowest at which a dealer may sometimes sell his goods, it is the lowest at which he is likely to sell them for any considerable time; at least where there is perfect liberty, or where he may change his trade as often as he pleases.

The actual price at which any commodity is commonly sold is called its market price. It may either be above, or below, or exactly the same with its natural price.

The market price of every particular commodity is regulated by the proportion between the quantity which is actually brought to market, and the demand of those who are willing to pay the natural price of the commodity, or the whole value of the rent, labour, and profit, which must be paid in order to bring it thither. Such people may be called the effectual demanders, and their demand the effectual demand; since it may be sufficient to effectuate the bringing of the commodity to market. It is different from the absolute demand. A very poor man may be said in some sense to have a demand for a coach and six; he might like to have it; but his demand is not an effectual demand, as the commodity can never be brought to market in order to satisfy it.

When the quantity of any commodity which is brought to market falls short of the effectual demand, all those who are willing to pay the whole value of the rent, wages, and profit, which must be paid in order to bring it thither, cannot be supplied with the quantity which they want. Rather than want it altogether, some of them will be willing to give more. A competition will immediately begin among them, and the market price will rise more or less above the natural price, according as either the greatness of the deficiency, or the wealth and wanton luxury of the competitors, happen to animate more or less the eagerness of the competition. Among competitors of equal wealth and luxury the same deficiency will generally occasion a more or less eager competition, according as the acquisition of the commodity happens to be of more or less importance to them. Hence the exorbitant price of the necessaries of life during the blockade of a town or in a famine.[2]

When the quantity brought to market exceeds the effectual demand, it cannot be all sold to those who are willing to pay the whole value of the rent, wages, and profit, which must be paid in order to bring it thither. Some part must be sold to those who are willing to pay less, and the low price which they give for it must reduce the price of the whole. The market price will sink more or less below the natural price, according as the greatness of the excess increases more or less the competition of the sellers, or according as it happens to be more or less important to them to get immediately rid of the commodity. The same excess in the importation of perishable, will occasion a much greater competition than in that of durable commodities, in the importation of oranges, for example, than in that of old iron.

When the quantity brought to market is just sufficient to supply the effectual demand and no more, the market price naturally comes to be either exactly, or as nearly as can be judged of, the same with the natural price. The whole quantity upon hand can be disposed of for this price, and cannot be disposed of for more. The competition of the different dealers obliges them all to accept of this price, but does not oblige them to accept of less.

The quantity of every commodity brought to market naturally suits itself to the effectual demand. It is the interest of all those who employ their land, labour, or stock, in bringing any commodity to market, that the quantity never should exceed the effectual demand; and it is the interest of all other people that it never should fall short of that demand.

If at any time it exceeds the effectual demand, some of the component parts of its price must be paid below their natural rate. If it is rent, the interest of the landlords will immediately prompt them to withdraw a part of their land; and if it is wages or profit, the interest of the labourers in the one case, and of their employers in the other, will prompt them to withdraw a part of their labour or stock from this employment. The quantity brought to market will soon be no more than sufficient to supply the effectual demand. All the different parts of its price will rise to their natural rate, and the whole price to its natural price.

If, on the contrary, the quantity brought to market should at any time fall short of the effectual demand, some of the component parts of its price must rise above their natural rate. If it is rent, the interest of all other landlords will naturally prompt them to prepare more land for the raising of this commodity; if it is wages or profit, the interest of all other labourers and dealers will soon prompt them to employ more labour and stock in preparing and bringing it to market. The quantity brought thither will soon be sufficient to supply the effectual demand. All the different parts of its price will soon sink to their natural rate, and the whole price to its natural price.

The natural price, therefore, is, as it were, the central price, to which the prices of all commodities are continually gravitating. Different accidents may sometimes keep them suspended a good deal above it, and sometimes force them down even somewhat below it. But whatever may be the obstacles which hinder them from settling in this center of repose and continuance, they are constantly tending towards it.

The whole quantity of industry annually employed in order to bring any commodity to market, naturally suits itself in this manner to the effectual demand. It naturally aims at bringing always that precise quantity thither which may be sufficient to supply, and no more than supply, that demand. . . .

Of the Principle of the Commercial, or Mercantile System

That wealth consists in money, or in gold and silver, is a popular notion which naturally arises from the double function of money, as the instrument of commerce, and as the measure of value. In consequence of its being the instrument of commerce, when we have money we can more readily obtain whatever else we have occasion for, than by means of any other commodity. The great affair, we always find, is to get money. When that is obtained, there is no difficulty in making any subsequent purchase. In consequence of its being the measure of value, we estimate that of all other commodities by the quantity of money which they will exchange for. We say of a rich man that he is worth a great deal, and of a poor man that he is worth very little money. A frugal man, or a man eager to be rich, is said to love money; and a careless, a generous, or a profuse man, is said to be indifferent about it. To grow rich is to get money; and wealth and money, in short, are, in common language, considered as in every respect synonymous.

A rich country, in the same manner as a rich man, is supposed to be a country abounding in money; and to heap up gold and silver in any country is supposed to be the readiest way to enrich it. For some time after the discovery of America, the first enquiry of the Spaniards, when they arrived upon any unknown coast, used to be, if there was any gold or silver to be found in the neighbourhood? By the information which they received, they judged whether it was worth while to make a settlement there, or if the country was worth the conquering. Plano Carpino, a monk sent as ambassador from the king of France to one of the sons of the famous Gengis Khan, says, that the Tartars used frequently to ask him, if there was plenty of sheep and oxen in the kingdom of France? Their enquiry had the same object with that of the Spaniards. They wanted to know if the country was rich enough to be worth the conquering. Among the Tartars, as among all other nations of shepherds, who are generally ignorant of the use of money, cattle are the instruments of commerce and the measures of value. Wealth, therefore, according to them, consisted in cattle, as according to the Spaniards it consisted in gold and silver. Of the two, the Tartar notion, perhaps, was the nearest to the truth.

.   .   .

It would be too ridiculous to go about seriously to prove, that wealth does not consist in money, or in gold and silver; but in what money purchases, and is valuable only for purchasing. Money, no doubt, makes always a part of the national capital; but it has already been shown that it generally makes but a small part, and always the most unprofitable part of it.

It is not because wealth consists more essentially in money than in goods, that the merchant finds it generally more easy to buy goods with money, than to buy money with goods; but because money is the known and established instrument of commerce, for which every thing is readily given in exchange, but which is not always with equal readiness to be got in exchange for every thing. The greater part of goods besides are more perishable than money, and he may frequently sustain a much greater loss by keeping them. When his goods are upon hand too, he is more liable to such demands for money as he may not be able to answer, than when he has got their price in his coffers. Over and above all this, his profit arises more directly from selling than from buying, and he is upon all these accounts generally much more anxious to exchange his goods for money, than his money for goods. But though a particular merchant, with abundance of goods in his warehouse, may sometimes be ruined by not being able to sell them in time, a nation or country is not liable to the same accident. The whole capital of a merchant frequently consists in perishable goods destined for purchasing money. But it is but a very small part of the annual produce of the land and labour of a country which can ever be destined for purchasing gold and silver from their neighbours. The far greater part is circulated and consumed among themselves; and even of the surplus which is sent abroad, the greater part is generally destined for the purchase of other foreign goods. Though gold and silver, therefore, could not be had in exchange for the goods destined to purchase them, the nation would not be ruined. It might, indeed, suffer some loss and inconveniency, and be forced upon some of those expedients which are necessary for supplying the place of money. The annual produce of its land and labour, however, would be the same, or very nearly the same as usual, because the same, or very nearly the same, consumable capital would be employed in maintaining it. And though goods do not always draw money so readily as money draws goods, in the long-run they draw it more necessarily than even it draws them. Goods can serve many other purposes besides purchasing money, but money can serve no other purpose besides purchasing goods. Money, therefore, necessarily runs after goods, but goods do not always or necessarily run after money. The man who buys, does not always mean to sell again, but frequently to use or to consume; whereas he who sells, always means to buy again. The one may frequently have done the whole, but the other can never have done more than the one-half of his business. It is not for its own sake that men desire money, but for the sake of what they can purchase with it.

. . .

Consumption is the sole end and purpose of all production; and the interest of the producer ought to be attended to, only so far as it may be necessary for promoting that of the consumer.

The maxim is so perfectly self-evident, that it would be absurd to attempt to prove it. But in the mercantile system, the interest of the consumer is almost constantly sacrificed to that of the producer; and it seems to consider production, and not consumption, as the ultimate end and object of all industry and commerce.

In the restraints upon the importation of all foreign commodities which can come into competition with those of our own growth, or manufacture, the interest of the home-consumer is evidently sacrificed to that of the producer. It is altogether for the benefit of the latter, that the former is obliged to pay that enhancement of price which this monopoly almost always occasions.[3]

It is altogether for the benefit of the producer that bounties are granted upon the exportation of some of his productions. The home consumer is obliged to pay, first, the tax which is necessary for paying the bounty, and secondly, the still greater tax which necessarily arises from the enhancement of the price of the commodity in the home market.

By the famous treaty of commerce with Portugal, the consumer is prevented by high duties from purchasing of a neighbouring country, a commodity which our own climate does not produce, but is obliged to purchase it of a distant country, though it is acknowledged, that the commodity of the distant country is of a worse quality than that of the near one. The home consumer is obliged to submit to this inconveniency, in order that the producer may import into the distant country some of his productions upon more advantageous terms than he would otherwise have been allowed to do. The consumer, too, is obliged to pay whatever enhancement in the price of those very productions, this forced exportation may occasion in the home market.

But in the system of laws which has been established for the management of our American and West Indian colonies, the interest of the home-consumer has been sacrificed to that of the producer with a more extravagant profusion than in all our other commercial regulations. A great empire has been established for the sole purpose of raising up a nation of customers who should be obliged to buy from the shops of our different producers, all the goods with which these could supply them. For the sake of that little enhancement of price which this monopoly might afford our producers, the home-consumers have been burdened with the whole expence of maintaining and defending that empire. For this purpose, and for this purpose only, in the two last wars, more than two hundred millions have been spent, and a new debt of more than a hundred and seventy millions has been contracted over and above all that had been expended for the same purpose in former wars. The interest of this debt alone is not only greater than the whole extraordinary profit, which, it ever could be pretended, was made by the monopoly of the colony trade, but than the whole value of that trade, or than the whole value of the goods, which at an average have been annually exported to the colonies.

It cannot be very difficult to determine who have been the contrivers of this whole mercantile system; not the consumers, we may believe, whose interest has been entirely neglected; but the producers, whose interest has been so carefully attended to; and among this latter class our merchants and manufacturers have been by far the principal architects. In the mercantile regulations, which have been taken notice of in this chapter, the interest of our manufacturers has been most peculiarly attended to; and the interest, not so much of the consumers as that of some other sets of producers, has been sacrificed to it.[4]

. . .

All systems either of preference or of restraint, therefore, being thus completely taken away, the obvious and simple system of natural liberty establishes itself of its own accord. Every man, as long as he does not violate the laws of justice, is left perfectly free to pursue his own interest his own way, and to bring both his industry and capital into competition with those of any other man, or order of men.[5] The sovereign is completely discharged from a duty, in the attempting to perform which he must always be exposed to innumerable delusions, and for the proper performance of which no human wisdom or knowledge could ever be sufficient; the duty of superintending the industry of private people, and of directing it towards the employments most suitable to the interest of the society. According to the system of natural liberty, the sovereign has only three duties to attend to; three duties of great importance, indeed, but plain and intelligible to common understandings: first, the duty of protecting the society from the violence and invasion of other independent societies; secondly, the duty of protecting, as far as possible, every member of the society from the injustice or oppression of every other member of it, or the duty of establishing an exact administration of justice; and, thirdly, the duty of erecting and maintaining certain public works and certain public institutions, which it can never be for the interest of any individual, or small number of individuals, to erect and maintain; because the profit could never repay the expence to any individual, or small number of individuals, though it may frequently do much more than repay it to a great society.

Smith's Notes

1. The natural or market price of commodities does not imply the quantity of gold or silver for which they will exchange, but their prices compared with each other, with labour, and with the necessaries of life, and other produce of soil or industry, of all which money is the common measure. By a very natural deception the prices are supposed to rise when gold and silver, the common measure, falls, although with respect to each other the different produce and manufactures retain their former proportion.

2. From this arises one essential difference, between articles of necessity and articles of taste or luxury, which appears in this, that it makes the value in use, and the value in exchange, the same thing, on some occasions, when the value in use regulates the value in exchange, and destroys all the ordinary laws of traffic and barter.

   Articles of the first necessity, (as the French term them), such as some sorts of eatables, are both of value in use and in exchange at all times. For farther illustration of this see the supplementary chapter on the price of grain.

3. As it has been so repeatedly asserted in this work, that every burthen laid on the producer, falls ultimately on the consumer, it would be fair to infer that every advantage granted to the producer is ultimately advantageous to the consumer, but the present assertions go directly to the contrary conclusion.—One or other of those conclusions must be wrong.

4. The idea that runs through the whole of the mercantile system, that is not a sufficient quantity of capital, and that every new channel robs the old one, has very much tended to injure the train of reasoning, which in other parts is admirable. Experience, and the evidence of facts, prove, however, in the most complete manner, that wherever a channel for trade is opened, capital is found, and that in place of a new branch of trade depressing others, all the branches have (with but very few exceptions) risen at one time. This has been the case in a remarkable degree, within the last ten or twelve years.

5. The economists are for giving a preference to agriculture; the author blames the legislature of this country, for wishing to prefer the mercantile interest, and he himself is for leaving them both entirely free.

Henry Carey: Essay on the Rate of Wages (1835)

Wealth of Nations was available in America from its first publication and undoubtedly had an early success because of its attack upon mercantilist restrictions on trade. The first American edition appeared in 1789; by 1820 there had been four other editions printed in the United States. Jefferson repeatedly recommended the work to younger acquaintances. In a letter to Thomas Mann Randolph, he declared Smith's *Wealth of Nations* "the best book extant" on political economy.

Henry C. Carey (1793–1879) was an early American economist who began his career as a disciple of Smith. The following selection from his *Essay on the Rate of Wages* (1835) was a defense of *laissez-faire* and an attack on the protective tariff. In his later work, Carey modified his position and became a protectionist, but his starting point in any argument was always Smith, who, to Carey, represented an authority who had to be answered. Even in this negative way, Carey demonstrated Smith's influence.

Adam Smith asserted that the rate of wages was regulated by the proportion which the supply of labour bore to the demand; a theory which has been controverted by writers of our time, on the ground that in no case where an article can be freely produced can

From Henry C. Carey, *Essay on the Rate of Wages* (Philadelphia: Carey, Lea, & Blanchard, 1835), pp. 7–9, 14–18.

any *permanent* influence upon price be produced by excess of demand, and that any rise must cause increased production that will sink the price again to the cost. That this argument is generally correct, there can be no doubt, but in order to make it fit man, it has been necessary to distort some facts, and overlook others, which are in direct opposition to it. Had subsequent writers followed the author of the Wealth of Nations, confining themselves to an examination of the various disturbing causes, the work of man, that operate among the several nations of the earth to produce the inequalities that exist in the proportion between the supply and demand, the "difficulty" would have been obviated.

There can be no difference of opinion as to the "importance" of this subject, and its peculiar importance at this time, when there is so strong a tendency to the transfer of the reins of government from the hands of the few to those of many. With the single exception of the United States, the privilege of making laws has heretofore been confined to certain classes, who, blinded by false views of their own interest, have generally acted as if government had been established for their peculiar benefit, and hence have arisen corn laws and monopolies of all kinds; restrictions on importations and exportations; wars, and their attendant, heavy taxation. It is not to be doubted, that many of those who promoted this system, have honestly believed that it was for the benefit of the nation over which they were placed; and that, with better information, they would have adopted a widely different course. They might, and probably would, have discovered, that *"laissez nous faire,"* the reply of the French merchants to Colbert, was sound and judicious; and that all that could be desired by any people of their government, was to let them alone, and confine its attention to the security of person and property; not allowing any man to "kick the shins or pick the pocket" of his neighbour with impunity. Had they done so, the governments of Europe would be deemed blessings, instead of curses, as is now too frequently the case. It remains to be seen, whether in those in which the people have attained a higher degree of influence than they have heretofore possessed, they will do better than has been done for them in times past by their hereditary lawgivers; and whether or not it will be so, depends upon a correct understanding of their own interests. If they can be made to see, that the course heretofore pursued has had a tendency to *depress* the rate of *wages*, and to keep the mass of the people in a state of poverty, it may be hoped that there will be a disposition to make trial of a different one, and ascertain its effects. If it can be shown that restrictions and monopolies—wars, and heavy taxation—low wages, poverty, and wretchedness—go hand in hand;—while free trade—freedom of action—peace—moderate taxation—high wages, and abundance, are all associated, there can be little doubt which will be their choice.

. . .

Had this subject been properly understood, we should long since have seen the end of protective tariffs; but as nothing can be more evident to the unenlightened than the advantage to be derived from making their neighbours pay them high prices, so nothing is more easy than to excite popular feeling in favour of a system of protection; and the same man who would deem absurd such a system in his own family, would advocate its adoption by the large family, termed a nation; as if those principles of trade which were true with regard to ten or twenty persons, could be untrue when applied to twenty thousand or two hundred thousand. It is a disgrace to our age to see two such nations as those of Great Britain and France each hedging round its commerce by restrictions that limit their exchanges to a million or two of pounds per annum; thus doing all in their power to frustrate the beneficent designs of the Deity, who, in giving to different parts of the earth different powers of production, paved the way for that intercourse which is most beneficial to mankind. "Commerce," says Mr. M'Culloch, "is the grand engine by which the blessings of civilization are diffused, and the treasures of knowledge and of science conveyed to the remotest corner of the habitable globe; while by making the inhabitants of each country dependent on the assistance of those of others, for a large share of their comfort and enjoyments, it forms a principle of union, and binds together the universal society of nations by the common and peaceful ties of mutual interest and reciprocal obligation."

In another point of view, it is highly desirable that it should be understood. *Wages and profits* have been represented by many political economists as natural antagonists, the Ormuzd and Ahriman of political economy, one of which could rise only at the expense of the other. Such has been the belief of the great mass of the people who receive wages, which belief has given rise to trades' unions, so numerous in England, and obtaining in the United

States; as well as to the cry of *the poor against the rich*. A large portion of those who pay, as well as those who receive wages, believe that the rate is altogether arbitrary, and that changes may be made at will. To this belief we are indebted for the numerous "strikes," or "turns out" we have seen, the only effect of which has been loss to both employers and workmen.[1] Had the journeymen tailors of London understood the laws by which the distribution of the proceeds between the workman and the capitalist is regulated, they would have saved themselves and their employers the enormous loss that has arisen out of their recent combination, and would have retained their situations instead of seeing themselves pushed from their stools by the influx of Germans, who seized gladly upon the places vacated by their English fellow workmen. Believing, as they do, that their wages are depressed for the benefit of their employers, they believe also that those employers are bound to give them a portion of their profits in the advance of wages, when, in fact, the employers are also sufferers by the same causes which produce the depression, and are unable to advance them, however willing they may be. If the real causes of the depression were understood, instead of combining against their employers, they would unite with them to free their country from those restrictions and interferences which produce the effect of which they complain, and would thus secure permanent advantage, instead of a temporary advance of wages, which is all that can be hoped for from combination, even if successful, which is rarely the case. Fortunately, in the United States there have been fewer interferences, and there is therefore less to alter, than in any other country; and if the workmen and labourers could be made to understand the subject, they would see that the division between themselves and the capitalist, or the rate of wages, is regulated by a law immutable as are those which govern the motion of the Heavenly bodies; that attempts at legislative interference can produce only disadvantageous effects; and, that the only mode of increasing wages is by rendering labour more productive, which can only be accomplished by allowing every man to employ his capital and talent in the way which he deems most advantageous to himself. They would see that all attempts on the part of the capitalist, to reduce wages below the natural rate, as well as all on their part to raise it above that rate, must fail, as any such reduction must be attended with an unusual rate of profit to the employer, which must, in its turn, beget competition among the possessors of capital, and raise the rate of wages; while such elevation in any employment must reduce the rate of profit so far as to drive capital therefrom, and reduce wages again to the proper standard.

They should see in the fact that the great majority of the master workmen have risen by their own exertions to the situations they at present occupy, abundant evidence that nothing is wanting to them but industry and economy. They should desire nothing but freedom of actions for themselves, and that security both of person and property which prompts the capitalist to investment; and so far should they be from entertaining feelings of jealousy towards those who, by industry and economy, succeed in making themselves independent, that they should see with pleasure the increase of capital, certain that such increase must produce new demands for their labour, accompanied by increased comfort and enjoyment for them. With such a system the population of this country might increase still more rapidly than it has done; the influx of people from abroad might be triple or quadruple what it has been, and each successive year find the comforts of the labouring population in a regular course of increase, as the same causes which drive the labourers of Europe here, to seek that employment and support denied them at home, impel the capitalist to seek here a market for his capital, at the higher rate of interest which our system enables us to pay him with profit to ourselves. The great influx of foreign labour at the present time has caused some uneasiness, but without good reason. The capitalist should bear in mind that if the supply of labour did not keep pace with the growth of capital, the profits of the latter would be diminished; and the labouring classes should recollect that if the labourers remained at home the capital would probably remain with them, and that, at all events, *every man who, by his arrival in this country, increases the number of producers, and of competitors for employment, also increases the number of consumers or employers.* Such people consume nearly, if not quite, the whole amount of their wages, and are therefore employers to nearly the same extent that they are competitors. . . .

Carey's Note

1. From a pamphlet recently published by Mr. Pratt, in relation to Savings Banks, it is found, "that the few counties which exhibit a falling off in the

amount of their deposits are precisely those in which trades'-unions and turns-out have prevailed to the greatest extent. Among parts of the country where unions appear to have flourished at the expense of the savings banks, we may enumerate Derbyshire and Durham, in the latter of which there has been a decrease of 917 out of 3651 accounts. As might naturally be supposed, the waste of capital has occurred principally among the smaller and poor depositors; the diminution in the number of accounts under £50, being 719, and the decrease in sums below £100, amounting to 830 of the entire 917."

Index